Crazy...Or Something Else Entirely

A (Mostly) Secret Journey With Bipolar Disorder

Jillian DuMond

(with excerpts by family & friends)

Charleston, SC
www.PalmettoPublishing.com

Crazy…Or Something Else Entirely
Copyright © 2023 by Jillian DuMond

All rights reserved

Paperback ISBN: 979-8-8229-1150-5

To all the friends I lost along the way.

And to my ride-or-dies that stayed with me through it all.

Special thanks to some of the real MVP's—those who took time out of their exceedingly busy lives and helped me piece this story together:

Matt B.
Tyler B.
Jeffrey DuMond
Kensington E.
Aunt Britt
Mom
Jacob
Jenna
Jonah
Jourdan

Could simply not have done this without you all.
And to my silent brothers, Josh and Jules, who I know would've dedicated the time to write, if only they had some of it.

Also, a very special thanks to the people who helped make my dreams of publishing this book come true. Namely:

Gennie Adams
Reinaldo D'Amico
Dr. Franklin & Winda DuMond
Jeffrey DuMond
Rita Heathcotte & Rick Jackson
Veronica Kirkpatrick
(The late, great) Kathryn Record
Diamond Richards
Macy Snodgrass
Brian & Britt Stemme
Kathryn Stemme
Dr. Jennifer Stone & Lynn Scott
Brooke Weinzapfel & Buddy Swift
Robert & Mary Ann Weinzapfel

"Sometimes you just need to talk about something—not to get sympathy or help, but just to kill its power by allowing the truth of things to hit the air."
-Karen Salmansohn

"Bipolar disorder is a brain disorder that causes changes in a person's mood, energy, and ability to function. People with bipolar disorder experience intense emotional states that typically occur during distinct periods of days to weeks, called mood episodes. These mood episodes are characterized as manic/hypomanic (abnormally happy or irritable mood) or depressive (sad mood). People with bipolar disorder generally have periods of neutral mood as well. When treated, people with bipolar disorder can lead full and productive lives.

People without bipolar disorder experience mood fluctuations as well. However, these mood changes typically last hours rather than days. Also, these changes are not usually accompanied by the extreme degree of behavior change or difficulty with daily routines and social interactions that people with bipolar disorder demonstrate during mood episodes. Bipolar disorder can disrupt a person's relationships with loved ones and cause difficulty in working or going to school.

Bipolar disorder is a category that includes three different diagnoses: bipolar I, bipolar II, and cyclothymic disorder.

Bipolar disorder commonly runs in families: 80 to 90 percent of individuals with bipolar disorder have a relative with bipolar disorder or depression. Environmental factors such as stress, sleep disruption, and drugs and alcohol may trigger mood episodes in vulnerable people. Though the specific causes of bipolar disorder within the brain are unclear, an imbalance of brain chemicals is believed to lead to dysregulated brain activity. The average age of onset is 25 years old.

People with bipolar I disorder frequently have other mental disorders such as anxiety disorders, substance use disorders, and/or attention-deficit/hyperactivity disorder (ADHD). The risk of suicide is significantly higher among people with bipolar I disorder than among the general population."

(https://psychiatry.org/patients-families/bipolar-disorders/what-are-bipolar-disorders)

The following story is my bipolar journey as best I can remember it. There are several inaccuracies on the sequence of events (I apologize in advance); I also had trouble remembering the vast majority of my manic episodes. To fill in some of the blanks and correct some of the plot holes, I asked family and friends to write their versions of the events from the viewpoints of those witnessing my journey through lucid eyes.

Oh, what? There's a pre-built disclaimer on the Internet for these kinds of things? Cool. Okay, well here's that, too:

The stories in this book reflect the authors' recollection of events. Some names, locations, and identifying characteristics have been changed to protect the privacy of those depicted. Dialogue has been re-created from memory.

Alright. Now we're in business.

Additionally, to try and make up for my shortcomings as the narrator of my own story, I compiled a Bipolar Jams playlist: *BIPOLAR JAMS- A PLAYLIST BY YOURS TRULY (EXPLICIT)*

1. Manic (Coleman Hell)- 3:44
2. I Wanna Be Sedated (The Ramones)- 2:30
3. Manic Depression (Jimi Hendrix)- 5:13
4. Fix Me Now (Garbage)- 4:43
5. Papercut (Linkin Park)- 3:05
6. Paranoid Eyes (Pink Floyd)- 3:42
7. This is Gospel (Panic! At The Disco)- 3:08
8. Where Is My Mind (Pixies)- 3:52
9. Bipolar (Krizz Kaliko)- 4:07
10. Gasoline (Halsey)- 3:17
11. Be Calm (fun.)- 4:10
12. No Self Control (Peter Gabriel)- 3:53
13. Lithium (Nirvana)- 4:17
14. Girl Anachronism (The Dresden Dolls)- 2:56
15. Everybody Hurts (R.E.M.)- 5:21
16. I'm Gonna Show You Crazy (Bebe Rexha)- 3:28
17. The Becoming (Nine Inch Nails)- 5:32
18. I'm So Tired (The Beatles)- 2:03
19. I Don't Remember (Peter Gabriel)- 4:42

20. Ode to Sleep (Twenty-One Pilots)- 5:09
21. Needy (Ariana Grande)- 2:53
22. Psycho Killer (Talking Heads)- 4:21
23. Formula (Labrinth)- 1:32
24. Mad Sounds (Arctic Monkeys)- 3:35
25. Control (Halsey)- 3:33
26. Down In It (Nine Inch Nails)- 3:46
27. Manic (Plumb)- 3:58
28. Half (PVRIS)- 4:26
29. Road to Joy (Bright Eyes)- 3:55
30. A Better Son or Daughter (Rilo Kiley)- 4:23
31. Everybody's Got Something To Hide Except Me and my Monkey (The Beatles)- 2:25
32. Secrets (Mary Lambert)- 3:43
33. Medication (Garbage)- 4:08
34. Lithium Sunset (Sting)- 2:37
35. Paint It Black (The Rolling Stones)- 3:46
36. I'm Tired (Labrinth ft. Zendaya)- 3:30
37. Vincent (Don McLean)- 3:58
38. My Mind & Me (Selena Gomez)- 2:30

RUN TIME ~2.5 HOURS

And what is the purpose of writing this book? I've been asked more than once, so

I thought it might not be a bad idea to cover it.

Here are some of the reasons I wanted to jot this down:

1. To give a voice to people who go through life with bipolar disorder. It is not an easy task, especially for those whose mood swings are a constant roller coaster, those who are in and out of the hospital on a regular or semi-regular basis, those who battle with addiction and other diagnoses simultaneously, those who have a support system that doesn't understand what they're going through, those who don't have a support system at all. Living with bipolar disorder is not easy by any means, nor is it easy to talk about. I'm hoping this may serve as a conversation-starter and a comfort to those who feel no one "gets it". I get it.

2. To give those with bipolar disorder hope. I thought my diagnosis was a death sentence. I tend to be dramatic on occasion (so sue me), but I'm certain I'm not alone in this one. When di-

agnosed with a mental illness—
any one of them—it can feel as
if the rug has been pulled from
under your feet, and life will
never be the same again. I've
been amazed to find that life
can be exciting and full of adventure or even as humdrum and
"normal" as it was before, and I
wanted to be sure and illustrate
that for those who are being
diagnosed today and those who
were diagnosed and gave up hope
long ago. Life isn't over. It
just takes a little more effort
than it once did. But it can
be very, very close to normal
again. Even boring sometimes!
Trust me, when you go through
the chaos of mania, you'll see
boredom in a whole new light.

3.   To shine a light on our mental healthcare system. Granted,
it's only a flashlight and not a
spotlight, but the more we tell
our stories about our hospital
stays, the more chance we have
of making positive change happen. Mental health facilities
in the United States need some
serious work, and the louder we
are about it, the better.

4. Selfishly, I want to see more
    books on the shelves about bi-
    polar disorder that aren't clin-
    ical. I wish more books like
    this existed when I was going
    through my own hospitaliza-
    tions and recovery. Mostly what
    I found about bipolar disorder
    was clinical and boring. I fig-
    ured if I wrote my own story,
    there'd be one more non-clinical
    book on the shelf for a diag-
    nosed bipolar person or a family
    member to peruse.

5. Again, selfish of me, but I
    wanted to have my story out
    there, once and for all. I've
    been living with this not-total-
    ly-well-kept secret that con-
    stantly looms over me, and I
    want to just air it out. Every-
    one who reads my memoir will be
    on the same page about "what
    happened" to me, and there will
    be no more speculation. Just the
    truth. As much of it as I can
    remember, anyway.

6. As a reference for—not only
    those with bipolar disorder,
    but also—those who know someone
    struggling with it. It doesn't

give all the answers, especially considering the fact that each diagnosis is one of a kind; however, it can give a glimpse into what bipolar disorder means for your loved one, and hopefully give some comfort and, even better, some advice.

7. To give a voice to my family and friends, who have battled my bipolar disorder as heartily as I have. I wanted to hear their sides of the story in addition to sharing with them my own version of events. It's been amazing to see this story take shape and come together with each individual's experience. We've learned so much about what it can feel like for each person to go through this journey, no matter how directly or indirectly, how nearly together or distant, and how each person's process has played a part and shaped my life since this diagnosis.

And now, without further ado,

CHAPTER ONE

How much of the journey do you really remember? It's foggy at best.

This is stupid, you're stupid, why are you doing this? Who is going to want to read it?

No one needs a book to tell them you're crazy.

I stare at the blinking cursor on the screen, my fingers frozen in place on the keys as a myriad of thoughts bounces around, each one trying to be first in line.

What if you start with some of the horrific hospital tales?

Oh, that's rich. As if you can remember any of those.

Besides, why immediately depress your audience? All 10 of them, that is.

Hey now.

Truth is, it's impossible to decide how and where to begin when writing about something as confusing and chaotic as a journey with bipolar disorder. If you or anyone close to you has a diagnosis, then you are well aware.

There are countless mental illnesses wholly misunderstood by the general public (the portion that has no personal experience with them, that is), and bipolar disorder is one of the most flagrant. Even growing up, before I had any hint of a diagnosis, I remember kids in my class calling each other "Bipolar" if someone was quick to anger. I *still* scroll Twitter and see full-blown adults referring to someone who *changes their mind* on a subject as "Bipolar". It regularly gets thrown around willy-nilly without people having the faintest idea of what it entails.

Who better to paint a picture of the disease for you than someone with the diagnosis, right? Damaged goods, reporting for duty.

That's a joke. Mostly.

I suppose I should offer a disclaimer: Being diagnosed bipolar has resulted in a warped sense of humor for me (Even more so than it was when I was Sane Jillian. I'm now Jillian, the artist formerly known as Sane). If you've ever lived through a manic episode as I have—complete with psychosis, hallucinations ... you know, the **works**—you've lived without dignity for however long the episode continued. And if you've lived without dignity, you know there's not much lower you can go. So, things become … *funny* in the darkest sort of way. Like laughter at a funeral.

To put it plainly, if I don't laugh about things, I'll most likely fall into a heap of self-pity, and that just isn't any way to live, is it? It isn't. So, I laugh. Most of the time.

If you find my jokes offensive, I have options for you as a recourse:

> Option 1: Close the book, put it down, and then do not pick it back up. Gift it to someone you don't want to spend money on for Christmas. You'll have to do a hard sell that you *couldn't put it down*, or they'll hate you forever. Good luck.

> Option 2: Continue reading, rolling your eyes at my jokes, until you can't take it anymore. Launch the book out the nearest window a la Bradley Cooper in *Silver Linings Playbook*. (A brief aside: I almost died when I saw Ernest Hemingway's name on the screen. I thought FOR SURE it had to be *The Old Man and the Sea*. Terrible book. I will never be convinced otherwise.)

Option 3: Go to Amazon. Search "Sense of Humor". Click "Add to cart". Proceed with purchase.

I will not be offended by any option chosen.

If you can't get on board with laughing about bipolar disorder, that's cool. It can be hard to laugh sometimes; it takes you to some pretty dark places, and I fully understand. I will say, from the bottom of my heart, I am laughing *with* bipolar disorder and not *at* it.

... Okay yes, that is a pun, but I am also being sincere. I still occasionally find it difficult to listen to my family members laughing about things I did while in episodic states. The humiliation lives on to this very day.

It's akin to that feeling of someone making fun of your family, right? They're more often than not repeating something they heard YOU say about them, but THEY'RE not allowed to say it. That's YOUR family.

It's MY illness. So even though *I* can make fun of my episodes, as I know exactly where the line not to cross is situated, others can only make fun of them *to a point*. Is that hypocritical? Yes, absolutely. But the waters surrounding mental illness are often murky, the ice thin, the territories uncharted. If someone tells you it hurts them to laugh, listen to them. Easy as that.

Unfortunately, this book is already in print, so if you're not ready to laugh a little, maybe come back to it another time. My journey has taken me to less than pleasant places, and I get it. Things become grim fairly quickly.

If it helps to know, there are entire portions that are terribly unfunny. Whether that's due to the subject matter or my jokes falling flat, who's to say? We may never know.

I typed all this, and my thoughts are still bouncing around and arguing about how to dive in.

Maybe you should just start with how it all began.

… Do you know where it began?

Clearly, I don't know what I'm doing.

If that is not the most apt description of my life to this point, I don't know what is. I will say, I recall life being far more comfortable *before* my diagnosis in the B.C. years (Before Crazy. The B.C. years encompass anything occurring before July 2014. Beyond that, we get into the A.D. years—After Diagnosis.). Not that everything as I knew it before being diagnosed was all rainbows and butterflies. I mean, maybe I still didn't know what I was doing, but I wasn't crazy … for lack of a better term.

I imagine for a great deal of people, a diagnosis can be a relief. That feeling of "I knew *something* was off, but I didn't know what. Now I have a term for it and a path to follow."

Unfortunately, not my case, but I really am happy for those of you who get to feel that way. It's always preferable to go from Point A of things-making-zero-sense to Point B of things-falling-into-place-and-making-perfect-sense as opposed to the reverse.

Personally, my diagnosis hit like a ton of bricks.

I also did not accept it, not at first.

It's indeed a trend among the bipolar community to respond to a diagnosis with, "Hmm, no I don't think so," at LEAST once. It's practically an initiation rite. I've joined the club. Guilty as charged.

Another fun trend in the bipolar community? To start feeling better on medications and decide we've been miraculously healed.

If you or someone you know has bipolar disorder and are currently not taking medications because you (or they) feel better, buckle up because I have news for you:

As of writing this, in the year of our Lord 2022, bipolar disorder can be treated, it cannot be cured. If you feel better, that means the medication is working. It will not continue working if you do not continue taking it.

This may seem obvious, but there is nothing the majority of those diagnosed bipolar want more than to just be normal again.

I speak from experience.

But please, take your medicine.

I'll be honest with you, I'm not on mine right now. I can't continue lecturing you as though I'm not a total hypocrite for not practicing what it is I'm preaching. For what it's worth, there is a solid reason I stopped, and it isn't that I'm cured. I may get into it later, I may not. I accepted before I paused it, though, that I would have to get back on it. It's a life-long type of thing currently, and it may just be that way forever. It really, really sucks. *ESPECIALLY* with the side effects. Believe you me, I know. But you can either take your medicine and feel functional or not take it and know you'll spend most of your life in a hospital. Or worse.

Personally, I don't know what's worse than the hospital, but I'm sure it's out there.

I digress.

I used to get notes from my teachers in high school that my writing lacked focus.

Joke's on you because my whole brain lacks focus, ya jerks.

To be fair, I didn't have the actual diagnosis (or experience any symptoms, for that matter) until after college. You know, when I was supposed to be marching into the "real world". Tell me it isn't a little hilarious:

"Look out world, here I come!"

LOL NO, BITCH, YOU CRAZY.

"But I'm trying to take on the world."

YOU'LL BE LUCKY TO TAKE ON THE NEXT HALF HOUR. LET THE GAMES BEGIN.

"… but I'm supposed to be an adult now."

LOLOLOLOLOLOL ENJOY THE HOSPITAL.

Reader, I did NOT. Enjoy. The hospital.

CHAPTER TWO

This is where, if my writing didn't lack focus, I would be launching into what the hospital was like since I clearly set up that segue.

Not only does my writing lack focus, but so does my brain in a manic episode. In essence, when I tell you that I mostly don't remember my hospital stays, I mean it. Candidly speaking, I don't know how much of that is my brain protecting me from reliving the worst days of my life to date, or if they're truly memories that are gone forever. I can give you the tableaus of my hospital stays that I remember, and I will. They're not pretty, and they certainly don't paint a complete picture.

I'm not ready to do that just yet. I've given you no exposition, and you have no inkling of what a manic episode is like. So let me give you a little backstory of my diagnosis first. We'll get into that hospital trauma later. It'll be fun.

I experienced my first manic episode mere months after my 22nd birthday and my graduation from college. I completed a performing contract in Virginia, I returned home to Indiana, and I promptly plunged right into uncontrollable mania within weeks.

Now, I'm not able to divulge what bipolar disorder is like across the board; every bipolar diagnosis is that whole mantra you hear about fingerprints and snowflakes. They're all different, individual, unique … however you want to put it. For instance, some with bipolar disorder are constantly cycling up and down, up and down. Mania, depression, mania, depression. I don't envy you. If that's your brand of bipolar disorder, I am sorry. I cannot imagine what it is like to go a day in your shoes. My own experience with bipolar disorder feels like Diet Bipolar Disorder or Bipolar Disorder Lite™ compared to yours. And mine is terrible, so I can't fathom yours.

As there are also multiple TYPES of bipolar disorder, allow me to be a tinge more specific about my own. I have a diagnosis of Bipolar Disorder I. It is, as I've read, the most severe form of bipolar disorder. Essentially, a home run on the first go-round. Go hard or go home, am I right?

You betcha. I can be a bit of an overachiever. A perfectionist if you will.

And boy did I perfect the art of mania right out of the gate. My manic episodes go a little something like this:

Monday: Fine.

Tuesday: Fine.

Wednesday: Decidedly less fine.

Wednesday afternoon: Full-blown mad.

Thursday: Incoherent.

Friday: Hospitalized. Until further notice.

It SWOOPS in like a bat out of Hell. There are warning signs, but they can be easy to miss if you don't know what to look out for.

Also, to clarify, there is only so much awareness happening in a person diagnosed bipolar who is already in the process of nosediving straight into a manic episode. It is truly up to the people in that person's immediate circle to watch for those glaring red flags. This doesn't absolve me from being aware of my surroundings and, say, keeping track of how much sleep I'm getting, for example; it just alerts the people surrounding me they'll have to be on the lookout if I start acting "off".

For me, the first warning sign (or "trigger", as you may hear them referred to) is a lack of sleep. If I go more than 24 hours without getting any sleep, there's a storm a brewin'. Especially if I say the words "I'm not tired," after having gone 24+ hours without sleep. It's entirely possible I'm already too far gone. It really doesn't take much disruption in the sleep cycle to spiral out of control ... at least not in my experience.

This trigger was tricky to distinguish for me. I've been a light sleeper for, well, pretty much my entire life. If I got 5 to 6 hours a night, I was set to take on the next day. I preferred to get the full 8 hours, but I could make do on at LEAST 5. It wasn't unusual for me, I should say, to function on less than the "normal" amount of sleep for the vast majority of my life.

In addition to that first trigger, if 24+ hours without sleep happens in July (especially mid-late July), you can bet there's a problem. Fun fact: Manic episodes are more likely to occur in the late summer. Why, you ask? I don't have any idea. It's just what I read. And experienced. Let me find some sources on it and get back to you.

Dear Google, why do manic episodes happen in late summer?

According to the Psychological Care and Healing Center:

"What's the connection? Bipolar disorder is a common type of mood disorder characterized by alternating states of elevated mood, or mania, and depression. As previous research has shown, extreme 'mood swings' in bipolar disorder have been strongly associated with disruptions in circadian rhythms – the 24-hourly rhythms controlled by our body clocks that govern our day and night activity.

Because warm temperatures tend to coincide with the longer days of summer, it may be that people are more likely to stay up later, in general, or have trouble sleeping in the heat, and this is what sets off the changes in brain chemistry that worsen symptoms. Or it could be the heat itself that brings about brain changes — or something else entirely.

Source:
https://www.news-medical.net/news/20120711/Daily-temperature-linked-to-bipolar-admissions.aspx

Circadian study:
https://www.eurekalert.org/pub_releases/2012-03/uom-bcm031312.php "

(The URL for this page is *https://www.pchtreatment.com/warm-weather-trigger-bipolar-disorder/* in case you wanted to go and see it with your own eyes.)

"Or something else entirely." So sciencey. It could be this, or it could be any number of other things triggering your episode.

Thanks for clearing that up with that extremely vague notion. Brilliant.

So, if I'm not sleeping, and it's mid-late July, there's DEFINITELY a problem. What about my cycle? Am I ovulating? Because that can ALSO be an issue for bipolar women. Those godforsaken hormones.

For the record, all three of these occurred recently, and—as I disclosed earlier—I'm not on medication. Am I in a manic episode right now? Who knows? We'll find out together when my writing stops making any sense. Voilà! A memoir just also became a suspense novel.

You know how I *hate* to get off topic (wink), but there is something that truly pisses me off about my brand of bipolar disorder that I just have to get off my chest. I mean, for the most part I really lucked out, so don't get me wrong. The fact that I am not in constant mood swings is most certainly a blessing, and I don't want to sound *too* ungrateful. However.

There are numerous sources of prominent people being dubbed "artistic geniuses" (sometimes self-ascribed, I imagine) who are diagnosed bipolar. Bipolar disorder has a way of concentrating itself in the brains of artists. Funny, that. Musicians, painters, actors, composers, etc. etc. All saying pretty much the same thing:

I have my best ideas when I'm manic. I hate to be on medication because it quashes my creativity.

Boy, do I feel cheated. I am, without a doubt, **NOT** a creative genius when I am manic. I go straight from average to *ab solutely insane* in a matter of hours with zero "Genius Phase" in between. So. I would like to speak to a manager.

That's right, I'm going to Karen my way out of this diagnosis.

To be fair, most of the artists praising their mania for their genius are usually referring to *hypomania,* which is a different phenomenon entirely. Hypomania is a much milder form of mania. In essence, energy levels may be higher than normal for a few days, and in most cases the hypomanic won't have to be hospitalized for it.

Just thought that could use some clarification. Anyway. Back to it then.

I have the most severe form of bipolar disorder (Type I) and my manic episodes come flying in with some signs, but they're quick. One misstep and BAM! Hospital. I had my first episode at 22 (July 2014). I don't believe I was properly diagnosed until I was closer to 23. It's foggy, so I'll have to think back on it. Or scrounge up my records. More reliable source of information. Kind of.

To be frank, most of my hospital records are only marginally more reliable than my manic-brain memory. A disappointing albeit factual circumstance, to say the least. Mental healthcare leaves much to be desired in the States, and I imagine that's something of a global phenomenon.

I'll become the Carmen Sandiego of mental facilities and find out. (A dated reference ... sorry Gen Z, I'm old. Google it.)

I wouldn't even wish that on my worst enemy, I am 100% kidding.

You know what, I've been doubly played, though. Another tangent, I apologize, but not only do I not have any kind of "Genius Phase", I also had zero indication before being diagnosed that I would one day be bipolar at all. For most cases of bipolar disorder, there's a genetic indicator, you know, it's hereditary. My grandparents don't appear to have dealt with it. Neither of my parents have it, nor do any of my six biological siblings (At least, not yet. Knock on wood.). I have several immediate family members that suffer from depression and anxiety ... and I've read that depression can be a factor. The thing about depression running in families, though, is that it still isn't indicative of whether someone will spontaneously turn out bipolar.

You can't prepare for something you don't know you need to be on the lookout for.

I do have one great-aunt with a diagnosis of Bipolar II. So, no direct lineage; no one other than my grandmother's sister, who has a less severe form. To me, it seems a little far-removed for it to be a causal genetic link, but what do I know? I'm not a doctor or scientist.

All I know is, I had to learn the hard way that I shouldn't have been put on an SSRI (Celexa), but there was not even a faint whisper of a clue that it was going to result in a manic episode. Up until the moment it did.

During my final year of college, I was unbearably anxious and depressed. I struggled with anxiety and depression off and on beginning in middle school, and by this point I felt it went untreated long enough. There's only so many times you can hear, "Try going for a walk or sleeping it off," before you decide, "Maybe that isn't working." An SSRI (namely, Citalopram aka Celexa) held promise for me. The Celexa seemed to be helping, and I ingested it for several months before it resulted in anything amiss.

An SSRI, by the way, is a "Selective Serotonin Reuptake Inhibitor". SSRIs treat depression by increasing serotonin levels in the brain.

Something that isn't widely known about SSRIs—sometimes even within the medical community (and especially those unfamiliar working with bipolar patients)—is that they can increase risk for manic episodes for those prone to them.

Why? How? All good questions. According to Psychiatry Advisor (Google with another save):

"Antidepressants "have the propensity to destabilize mood, precipitating both hypomanic and manic episodes"—a phenomenon called antidepressant associated hypomania (AAH).[1] Although this condition is most frequently associated with bipolar depression, it has also been reported in unipolar depression and in non-affective conditions, such as anxiety disorders.[1] The potential for AAH has made antidepressant use controversial in patients with bipolar disorder (BP).[2] "

It goes on:

"The authors state that AAH has been attributed to several different causes.

- An "iatrogenic, reversible affect of antidepressants, which abates on cessation of the drug";[3,4]

- A "discrete form of BP" (sometimes labeled bipolar III disorder) in which hypomania or mania only occur in the setting of antidepressant treatment;[4]

- Conversion from unipolar depressive disorder to BP attributable to the antidepressant;[5]

- "Acceleration in the natural course of an underlying but then emerging bipolar condition";[6]

- A "coincidental phenomenon" unrelated to antidepressant treatment, which might occur in someone with "pseudobipolar" disorder, as part of a "nascent" bipolar I disorder (BP1) or bipolar II disorder (BPII).[7,8]"

(https://www.psychiatryadvisor.com/home/ depression-advisor/antidepressant-associated-hypomania-navigating-clinical-challenges/)

That's right. If one has a predisposition to mania, SSRIs are not going to be beneficial in most cases.

To take it a step further, if one has a predisposition to mania, and DOESN'T KNOW IT, and is prescribed SSRIs, one is going to—how best to put it—fuck around and find out. Pardon the French.

Celexa was great until it was most assuredly not, but I can't give the SSRI all the credit. I should also thank all my friends and online sources telling me marijuana is not at all dangerous and has zero negative effects. While that is true for some, that is not true for Jillian. I have yet to have a manic episode without any traces of weed in my system.

And no, you do not have to smoke heavily to walk into a full-blown manic episode. Leading up to my first episode, I was smoking the resin at the bottom of the bowl, only one or two tokes a night. Plus the Celexa in the morning.

Let's look at the math on my first episode:

2 tokes marijuana/night + 80 mg of Celexa + Late summer = MANIA

Now. That said, 80 mg of Celexa is twice the maximum daily dosage. Why would I do that? I'd love to tell you. Because I was 22 years old. And 22-year-olds can be so very dumb. I already smoked to go to sleep that night, realized I forgot my medication (40 mg/day) that morning, and, *instead of skipping it as I should have,* I took twice the amount to make up the difference. Because math.

Suffice it to say, my sanity was not long for the world that night.

The math on my second manic episode—occurring in July 2020 (notice that trend? July?)—looks like this:

Marijuana (1x/week) + Quarantine (in dangerous area …ever heard of Panorama City?) + Late summer (Endless Los Angeles fireworks + No sleep) = MANIA

As you can see, with that second episode, I didn't stand a chance. It was a perfect storm with every possible factor working against me. Including myself with the smoking. But there's an explanation for why I picked it back up, albeit not a good one.

I thought I was in the clear.

See, because I had that trendy "No, I don't think I'm bipolar" moment, but my "moment" lasted a full 5+ years of unmedicated normalcy. A blissful, beautiful 5+ years full of hope and optimism, completely dashed by reality when the crazy reared its ugly head in a brutal comeback.

Hence, thus, ergo. The need for exposition.

So, to recap, I have a diagnosis of Bipolar I. I experienced my first manic episode at 22, when I was taking an SSRI for depression/anxiety and smoking marijuana, which resulted in mania. I was not properly diagnosed until I was closer to 23. I subsequently halted medication and had 5+ years with zero complications until my second episode in 2020 (at age 28). I had no genetic indication prior to *any* of it (other than one great-aunt with Bipolar II) that I was prone to bipolar disorder to begin with.

So how did I end up bipolar at all? I've touched on what *triggers* my episodes, but *how* am I bipolar?

Let's look at the reasons someone might be diagnosed. We'll let the Mayo Clinic take this one:

"Causes
The exact cause of bipolar disorder is unknown, but several factors may be involved, such as:

- Biological differences. People with bipolar disorder appear to have physical changes in their brains. The significance of these changes is still uncertain but may eventually help pinpoint causes.

- Genetics. Bipolar disorder is more common in people who have a first-degree relative, such as a sibling or parent, with the condition. Researchers are trying to find genes that may be involved in causing bipolar disorder.

Risk factors
Factors that may increase the risk of developing bipolar disorder or act as a trigger for the first episode include:

Having a first-degree relative, such as a parent or sibling, with bipolar disorder

Periods of high stress, such as the death of a loved one or other traumatic event

Drug or alcohol abuse"

(To see for yourself, you can go to *https://www.mayoclinic.org/diseases-conditions/bipolar-disorder/symptoms-causes/syc-20355955*)

As I put it a chapter ago, I'm damaged goods. I have an inexplicable "biological difference". Which, DUH.

"Hm there's something different going on here. Did you get a haircut?"

Could it be that I'm strapped to a hospital bed because I'm in and out, but mostly out, of sanity? Just a guess.

CHAPTER THREE

If you or someone you know has bipolar disorder, there's no question you've seen a manic episode. However, unless you personally have had one, you can't know what it's like. Period. You need to understand that, so allow me to emphasize it:

Even if you've directly seen someone have a manic episode, you have no idea what it's like from the inside.

I'm going to try my best to piece together what I can recall from my own manic episodes to give you an *impression* of what it's like.

Have you ever been "blackout" intoxicated? If you haven't, lemme tell ya, it is unpleasant. You have little to no awareness of what is going on around you; your senses are entirely dulled. But you're still walking, still talking, still trying to distinguish or perceive what's happening. And of course, everyone around you knows you're intoxicated, there's no question.

They may not know *how* intoxicated, but there's no denying that you aren't sober. It usually lasts a handful of hours until it dissipates by one or a combination of the following:

1.   Drinking a TON of water and draining it out,

2.   Vomiting it out, and/or

3.   Sleeping it off and making do with a massive hangover.

Most young adults leave college with at least one "Blackout" story (which, typically, other people have to piece together for them). If one comes to mind, then you have some semblance of the lack of awareness happening during a manic episode.

Now imagine being "blackout" but stone cold sober. And instead of having your senses dulled, they're heightened. But even though you feel as though you're processing everything more quickly than ever before, your brain is a runaway train, and you can't keep up. And imagine that it lasts, not only hours, but days. Weeks.

It starts as an incredible amount of energy. You can't stop walking, shuffling, dancing around the place. You can't sit still. Too much energy. Can't sleep. Not tired. Just moving.

Your thoughts start picking up steam. You've got a lot going on in your brain. Lots to talk about. But who are you going to tell? You will tell LITERALLY ANYONE. Family, friends, coworkers, vague acquaintances, complete strangers, you'll tell anyone who will listen. You must get it all out right now. There's so much running through your thoughts, you feel like you're in overdrive.

You're making connections that no one can keep up with. Thoughts that seem unrelated, words that come from anywhere and everywhere you've ever heard or seen them. Movie quotes, music lyrics, a joke you heard once when you were 10, a YouTube video you saw in college, something you learned in a high school history class, an anecdote from a lifetime ago—did it even happen?, a hymn from the church you haven't attended in 10+ years … anything your brain can scrounge up. Jumping from point to point, synapses firing, and why do they look so confused? It's all connected, it always has been.

You start seeing more vibrant colors and hearing sounds differently. The sun is overwhelming, cars are deafening. Every song you turn on makes so much *sense*. You try to explain it, but it comes out a jumble of ideas and sentence fragments. And your brain is retaining none of it. You're processing it all differently, strongly, but nothing is sticking. It's all a mish-mash of light, sound, smell, touch, what is happening? Not a clue.

You still aren't tired. Are you crying? Why? You don't know. You try to talk about it. You don't make any sense. That's hilarious, now you're laughing. Still not making any sense, but you're rolling, bubbling with laughter, tears still on your face from moments ago when you were unbearably sad. A hodgepodge of emotions to go with your hodgepodge of thoughts. Hodgepodge is a fun word, isn't it? Hodgepodge, hodgepodge, hodgepodge …

And do you know what's happening? Not even in the slightest. Your brain is full steam ahead, crashing and burning, rapidly thinking and thinking and thinking with absolutely nothing sticking in one place. It's all echoes and noise and did someone just say something? You can't hear anything over the deafening thoughts screaming at you. You don't know what you're doing, you don't know what you're saying, you're just doing you. And you is batshit crazy.

Wait, maybe you should post it online. You're famous, after all (Delusions of grandeur have come into play, naturally.). You start posting your ideas, your thoughts, making live streams. Have you ever made live streams before? No. But you've never had such important thoughts, you'll figure it out. Wait, what does this button do? It'll be fine, just keep clicking buttons until the thing you want to happen happens. Is the government tracking your every move? Probably. Whatever, let them. (That's just in your head, too, by the way. Because paranoia will also float around just for kicks. But you won't know that.)

Your ideas are out of control. You're losing track of time, of sleep, of food, of water. You don't have words anymore; you can't remember your own name. You can't see anything happening in front of you. It's both painfully bright and a total blur. Still no sleep. Still no rest. When did you last eat? No clue. No time. So many thoughts. Hallucinations. Your thoughts and words are racing, racing, racing. No end in sight.

Anything beyond this point—and most everything leading to it—is an empty void in your memory.

The only saving grace of mania.

You eventually wake up in a hospital. *Where am I and how did I get here?* Remnants of hospital beds and needles-of-who-knows-what and intake nurses are floating around in your memory. And then you're KNOCKED OUT. And when you come to, other than some tiny glimpses and fragments, you can't recount the last few hours, let alone the last week.

Someone else will eventually inform you that you told them the guy on the TV was coming to blow up your house. That you unplugged everything at 3 in the morning because you were afraid the house was going to explode. That you thought you had magical powers and were mixing "potions". That you hitchhiked to a bar. That you spent hundreds, maybe thousands, of your savings. That you grabbed a knife and tried to walk outside with no explanation. Your friends are alienated, you've humiliated yourself, drained your savings, and you have to start everything over from scratch.

Again.

Welcome back.

Mania is a lot more fun in the *during* phase than in the aftermath. During the mania, you're primarily beside yourself with euphoria. Extremely, furiously, maddeningly, overwhelmingly happy with utterly zero explanation … and zero idea of what's happening, of course.

There are some decent film/television examples if you have no personal experience and wish to see a vague idea of a manic episode in action. In my opinion, the show *Homeland* with Claire Danes does the best job of depicting a manic episode, but that could also be because it's the closest I've seen to resembling my own. I thought Zendaya's portrayal during *Eupho-*

ria was also respectable, but her character's brand of bipolar disorder was far more cyclical than mine. Also, the show focused more on her struggle with addiction than her bipolar diagnosis. Admittedly, the two are often hand in hand—bipolar disorder and addiction. *Silver Linings Playbook* might have had a strong interpretation with Bradley Cooper's character, but bipolar disorder manifests differently between males and females, so it's hard for me to say.

Side note: Most Hollywood film/television productions portraying anything akin to a mental facility romanticize them, more often than not, which boggles my mind. Of all things to sentimentalize … psych wards? Really?

Simply bizarre.

My own, personal brand of bipolar goes from normal to MANIC AF to very depressed (due to the aftermath of the manic episode and the side effects of the drugs) to eventually back to Normal Junior. I don't cycle often outside of manic episodes and Episode Aftermath, which is why it may be easier for me to fool anyone who doesn't know me personally into thinking I'm 100% sane across the board.

Suckers.

To clarify, I say Normal Junior (Please, Normal is my *father*.) because once it's made known that you're bipolar, you never

get to go back to Normal. Not in my experience. Maybe others have, and that's most
excellent. If you're one of those people
who's been able to go back to Normal, I
need you to reach out and tell me how that
happened. I'm on Facebook. Holla.

I must know all your secrets because
in my case, the people close to me are
watching me like hawks. Only because they
care, of course. I don't mean to knock
anyone for expressing concern. As previously stated, it is up to them to catch any
glaring issues in case I'm already too far
gone to do so myself. There is, however,
a delicate balance to maintain between
being cautious and being paranoid. Otherwise, from now on, any strong emotions
I have are *bipolar* strong emotions. Any
insomnia is *bipolar* insomnia. I don't have
just normal experiences as a human being
anymore, I am a *bipolar* human being, and
I MUST ALWAYS BE CAREFUL.

It can be frustrating, to say the least.
I don't like being met with "Are you on
your medicine?" because I became over-
whelmed and cried. Or because I ranted
about something upsetting and frustrating
in the world. Or because I couldn't fall
asleep one night. It's the bipolar equiva-
lent of "Is it your time of the month?"
but, like, for the rest of your life.

If you know, you know.

And it can be exceptionally isolating. I meant what I said when I wrote, "Your friends are alienated." I had several friends that I lost explicitly because of something I did or said while manic.

Being diagnosed, for me, is like I went to bed one person and woke up someone completely different. I didn't feel any different, but everyone around me (who knew what I'd been through) declared I was. And not always by using their words. Oftentimes, it's in a look: I've seen confusion, uncertainty, pity, occasionally fear. Sometimes it's in a new distance put between us, a deafening silence where there used to be laughter, and how-are-yous, and I-miss-yous.

One of the most eye-opening aspects of feeling as though I woke up completely different, however, is how in my own head it is … for the most part. There are times that, yes, the people around me treat me differently from before and/or see me as a different person, but there's an insane (ha) amount of people who still have no idea what I've gone through, who have no knowledge about this journey with bipolar disorder at all.

See, after I'd go through a manic episode, followed by hospitalization, I'd get that feeling—and I'm sure you've felt it before, too—that everyone would just know. Everyone would be able to look at me and see "Bipolar" stamped on my forehead. I'd never be the same, I'd never be able to hide it; my life as I knew it was over. It was that scarlet letter "A". It was that walk of shame on campus. I was the emperor without clothes. I was branded. The end.

And that simply is not the case.

I'm 100% certain there remains a goodly number of people who don't know about my diagnosis. Like, at all. They know something "weird" happened, but beyond that, *shrug*.

I haven't exactly been super loud and proud about it.

On the contrary, during my second episode, I was instead super loud and proud about *not* having a diagnosis. On Facebook live.

You read that correctly, DURING A MANIC EPISODE.

I can't think of a crueler irony.

But like I said, it's a little funny.

TYLER (COLLEGE FRIEND)

When Jillian told me she was bipolar ⋯ at first, I thought it was a joke.

It can be hard to tell with Jillian sometimes, whether she's joking around or not. I mean, I never saw or experienced anything other than the person I knew and was such good friends with in college, so I had a hard time understanding what it was she was referring to. She was still bitingly sarcastic, still a weird mix of completely serious and unserious, still ⋯ sane, it seemed to me.

I couldn't see anything to indicate a mental illness in her, not during or since college.

There wasn't anything that was helping me piece this confusing puzzle together.

Granted, I didn't know much about bipolar disorder on the whole, but nothing about the Jillian I knew gave me the impression that she was anything other than ⋯ fairly normal. Aside from a pretty bad breakup her junior year, I never knew her to swing into anything resembling depression. There were never any depressive or manic moods that would disrupt her entire life or incapacitate her. Nothing about her struck me as being someone that was emotionally unstable to the point that I felt like I needed to sleep with one eye open or something.

I mean, even with the chronic lack of sleep and the substantial amounts of alcohol (and sometimes marijuana) that we'd ingest during our college days ⋯ she didn't experience anything along the lines of what she's been through since.

For some reason, she's entrusted me to shed some light on what knowing her was like in the BC period (Before Crazy, as she says), but, like, the prehistoric BC period. Because yes, we're practically dinosaurs now—in our 30s and all, and no longer the idiot college kids we once were. From well before her diagnosis was even a blip on the timeline.

So, allow me to say, Jillian and I became friends in an unforgettable way ⋯ that neither of us can actually remember 100%.

College, you know?

It's funny—she and I took a trip down memory lane before I sat down to write this, and I was shocked to realize we couldn't remember how we became friends. And yet, it's one of my most-valued friendships from college. It's been able to withstand the tests of time, distance ⋯ a great many of the elements have come our way, but our friendship has somehow remained intact. We're usually able to pick up exactly wherever we leave off, and it's always a sarcastic, "Everything's good," but punctuated with a tone of, "Fuck my life," and an awkward laugh. We like to commiserate with one another, naturally, as misery loves company.

But it's never actually miserable. Because it's 99% sarcasm and 20% laughter.

I know what you're saying: Tyler, that's mathematically impossible.

I'm here to tell you I've learned nothing is impossible when it comes to my friendship with Jillian.

The first time Jillian and I worked directly together in our theatrical college ventures was during the spring semester of my sophomore year and her freshman year. We were both selected to be in our department's first show choir group: The Hilltopper Showstoppers. It was basically the college version of Glee. She distinctly remembers being laughed at by high school students when we'd "tour" and perform. I remember a standing ovation or two. Goes to show how each of us looks at things—I've always preferred to look on the bright side of life, and she's always ⋯ well, she certainly doesn't sugarcoat life, I can tell you that much. That isn't to say she's ever taking things too seriously, but more with a sick and twisted, dark sense of humor.

And brutal honesty.

I always found her candidness hilarious and refreshing. Typically, performers try to butter you up, kiss ass, get on your good side in the hopes of developing and maintaining a positive reputation. Jillian didn't bother playing by those rules. She was going to say EXACTLY what she thought, whether I liked it or not.

My senior year, she and I eventually found ourselves as housemates at a joint that we and our friends dubbed, "The Hive." (Basically, it was yellow ⋯ that was the long and short of the naming process.) There was a group of six of us musical theatre students living together under one roof.

Was it loud? Yes. Was it insane? Also, yes. Were Jillian and I somehow the LEAST insane? I'd have to poll our former housemates, but I'd be willing to bet we'd be dubbed the "Most Vanilla" (boring, quiet hermits) by a longshot.

So, I was kind of a shut-in while we were living at The Hive, even more than she was. I mean, it's not a competition, but if it was, I'd absolutely win because I was constantly BOOKED. The hustle felt non-stop (between work, classes, shows, etc.), so by the time I was finally able to be home, I wanted to just be in my room. Alone. Chilling in the quiet, doing what I wanted to do, working on what I wanted to work on.

Everyone else would be going to the bars, fre- quently hanging out, always socializing. I found this exhausting because of the constant lack of free time; Jillian found it exhausting because of the idea of having to be around people.

Sometimes, she would text a "Hey, what're you up to? Are you in your room again?" from the floor below and would force her and Kirby's (her dog's) presence upon me.

Not that I always minded.

When we elected to stay at home and hang out, I knew that whatever she and I talked about would be open, honest, hilarious, and would never leave the room. She was someone I could trust and someone who trusted me—a bit of a rarity in the theatrical world.

I also remember her being a *bit* of an instigator when we actually did venture into public, enjoying some shock value comedy at the expense of her unwitting "audience." For example, she'd talk me into staging fake, very dramatic and loud "breakups" just to entertain ourselves watching people's reactions. Or, as we were trudging our way up to the top of the hill where the Theatre & Dance (T&D) Department buildings were located, she'd drop something super embarrassing ("Hey how's your herpes?") as soon as people were walking by, etc.

Never a dull moment.

Once, I was hosting our department's annual "Fun" Cabaret that would commemorate the onstage/offstage drama of each year through inside jokes and performances; as the kids would say, we'd "spill the tea" onstage. Was everyone performing and/or attending sober? Who's to say? We may never know.

Ah, college.

In the days before the actual show, Jillian and I were shooting the shit per usual, when she said something in her typical, blunt fashion that must've rubbed me the wrong way because I wrote a song about it entitled, "Jillian Is a Bitch Today," as she was sitting there and listening to it. Couldn't say now whether illicit substances were at play or just the copious amounts of sleep deprivation we were miraculously still functioning on. I played the only 3 chords I knew at the time and wrote lyrics about Jillian being a bitch "in four different octaves." Most women I know would probably not find it quite so funny.

Not. Jillian.

She BEGGED me to play it during my hosting gig. It was hilarious for us both to watch the audience—comprised mostly of other T&D students—uncomfortably laugh and look around, unsure whether to find it funny or not, until they safely saw Jillian laughing her ass off in the front row.

How that drunken night became one of the only things both of us could easily remember, we may never know. (It was probably the award-winning song.)

I have so many fond memories of Jillian's and my friendship during our time at WKU and beyond, but even as I drag up every last, fuzzy one, nothing stands out for me as being that EUREKA! moment. Nothing that clicks and says, "Yes, there it is. That was when I could tell you were bipolar."

And believe me, I really sat down and gave it some thought. I wanted to make sense of what my friend was telling me. I wanted to understand.

And for the life of me, I couldn't make the pieces fit.

CHAPTER FOUR

I spent my four years of college pursuing and obtaining (after what felt like an eternity) my Bachelor of Fine Arts degree in Performing Arts with a Concentration in Musical Theatre. A ridiculous concept for a degree, I know, but I decided at a young age that I wanted to be an actor, and I never swayed from chasing what I felt was my calling. Not even after being told repeatedly it was a financially unstable career. Not even after being rejected over and over by my college professors and various directors on my "professional" journey. Not even after people assured me I would never "make it" (whatever that's supposed to mean).

Sometimes, though, even if you don't sway … life will sway for you.

My first manic episode is a blur of pixelated fragments. It happened nearly a decade ago, but I can remember bits and pieces, some clearer than others.

I returned home from my performing contract in Charlottesville, Virginia. I was fresh off the grill from a full summer of singing, dancing, smoking weed, drinking, and partying with my castmates. It happened to be my second "professional" (read: paid) theatrical contract, and I was in a celebratory frame of mind. What a way to begin the rest of my life as an actor.

Now back in Indiana, I was spending most of the evening on Facebook, creating a new "Acting Page". I was overflowing with excitement to be starting my acting career, and I spent hours tracking down footage to add. When I finally called it and decided it was time to go to bed, I smoked (as I had been doing nightly for weeks) to help put me to sleep and suddenly realized I had forgotten to take my Celexa earlier that morning. I took two to make up for the one I'd forgotten.

IDIOT.

I remember being on the phone with a friend from college. We'll call him DJ. I didn't know DJ terribly well; he was a newer friend, but we'd been talking a bit more lately, and I called him—after doubling my dose.

> "I'm afraid if I fall asleep, I'm going to die. I feel so weird. So floaty. Maybe I'm already dead. What if we're already dead? DJ, I don't know … if I fall asleep, I don't

> think I'm going to wake up again.
> I'm worried."

> "I'm coming to find you, hang on.
> Where are you?"

> "I live by a lake. I'm going to walk
> outside and meet you."

I couldn't recall my address, the one where I'd resided nearly my entire life to this point. I walked outside. It must've been around 2 or 3 in the morning. Maybe even closer to 4. *It's so dark out, but the air feels good. Warm. Breathe in, breathe out, breathe in, breathe out.*

DJ had also been smoking, and perhaps drinking, and he hopped in his car to come "find me". Something was clearly lost in translation because he didn't realize I was in Indiana. He was in Kentucky. He'd have a bit of a drive, but he had it in his mind, I think, that I was nearby. Don't ask me how, I'm only recounting this to you in the fragments I remember.

Unsurprisingly, DJ was pulled over, and suddenly a police officer was on the phone.

> "Where are you? Where are your par-
> ents?"

I remember telling him my dad was a doc-tor, and I have no idea what he said … I'm sure he was trying to advise me to find my parents. Because next thing I know, I'm driving to my dad's office. (Since my parents' divorce years before, I barely had any inkling of a relationship with my father, by the way, and my mother was asleep right upstairs. Did I just subconsciously know somehow that I needed medical attention? Your guess is as good as mine.)

Driving became a wildly fascinating experience. I turned the air in my car FULL BLAST and rolled the windows down. I never felt air on my face so strongly before. There were suddenly tears streaming from my eyes; the music made me cry. I don't remember what was so viscerally relatable, enough to draw tears. I couldn't tell you what song was playing now, but that isn't surprising. I wouldn't even have been able to tell you by the time I parked the car. I was going back and forth in body temperature from being very hot to very cold and the music felt like it was going from incredibly fast to incredibly slow; I was hearing the tempo differently, without the tempo of the song actually changing. The sun was only beginning its ascent, so there was a beautiful sunrise on my way there.

I don't know how I made it alive. Thank goodness for dual processing.

I arrived in the parking lot feeling very dizzy. I promptly parked, opened the door of my vehicle, and retched all over the pavement. (This turned out to be an exceedingly fortuitous event, since once I arrived at the hospital, no one thought it might be a good idea to pump my stomach.)

I left the door open, sat back in my seat, and closed my eyes. It wasn't until the first nurse arrived and ushered me inside that everything really took a turn.

I laid down on the couch in my dad's pediatric office, shivering and confused, afraid I was dying. My parents arrived on the scene and were trying to pump me for information about what was going on. I told them something along the lines of "The old me is dying," or some such metaphorical nonsense. No one knew how to help.

Still under the impression I was dying, I told them to make some calls to my siblings so I could apologize.

They humored me and made some telephone calls, and then they drove me to a psych hospital.

I vaguely remember intake. Very vaguely. I remember having visual hallucinations[*]. I could see all kinds of little shapes and figures moving in what appeared to me a

---

[*] I've since been told by my new psychiatrist, Dr. R _ _ _ , that these are not considered "hallucinations" but rather "illusions". Because "hallucinations" will happen even with your eyes closed, but "illusions" require light to play out. Learn new things about mental health every single day.

moving painting. According to my mother, it was a generic photograph of some trees.

Audio hallucinations started as well. At one point, when she was responding to a nurse's question, I heard my mother speaking German, and I laughed. *What is going on? Why is she speaking a different language here? I'm definitely dying.*

And then I was being walked through signing papers. I signed without any clue what was happening. Couldn't read them, didn't know what they meant. I'm sure the nurses were explaining everything, but I could hear nothing, I was figuratively underwater.

Voluntary, they say.

And then I was abruptly being led away by a gaggle of nurses, and I still think I'm dying the entire time, so I start throwing a fit because I don't want to go with them, and then I have NO IDEA what happened after that. According to my admissions report, I was walking around touching patients, telling them they were going to Heaven. (I'm not religious, by the way. I was raised Catholic, but that's a brand of Catholicism that's completely separate from the religion. Anyone who says they were "raised Catholic" is not a practicing Catholic. In essence, if I start talking about religious/churchy things, it's also a warning sign of a manic episode.)

Apparently, the nurses were *very* focused on the tidbit about me smoking marijuana—I suggested it must have been laced to be having such a bad effect (never mind that I'd been smoking it nightly for days, maybe weeks by this point). I don't know how effective I was at communicating that I had doubled up my dose of Celexa—or if I could even remember that happening, for that matter. Consequently, everyone focused on the weed intake.

And what does one do in order to test for toxic substances? One submits to a drug test. A urine sample.

These nurses decided it would be a sound idea to send me into a bathroom to take a urine sample. Alone.

Remember just a moment ago when I was having a manic episode?

Suffice it to say, the urine sample did not go according to plan. I'll try to spare you as many gruesome details as possible, but let's just say one second, I'm successfully conducting a urine sample, and the next, the cup has fallen into the toilet.

Shit.

What do you think a 22-year-old female (with no medical training) in the midst of her first manic episode is going to do in this case? Well, I'll tell you. She's going to try to fix the problem the only way she knows how.

She's going to put the urine back into the cup.

Does she understand that it's been tampered because it's totally diluted from the toilet water? No, of course not. Furthermore, the nurses don't understand she's having a manic episode and therefore believe she's trying to cheat the system.

When I tell you that this is how intake went, I assure you it did not become any more pleasant from there.

The thing I remember most distinctly is waking up and seeing my "roommate" sitting on her bed, staring at me. Just a vacant, empty stare. And I did not expect to wake up anywhere other than in my bedroom at home. Like it was all just a bad dream, and I would be back in my own bed. But that vacant, empty stare from a total stranger told me otherwise.

Uh-oh.

My roommate was not well. I know that's a severe case of the pot calling the kettle black, but when I decided to take a shower and assess my next steps, the towels were all over the floor and soaking wet, the toilet paper was drenched … the entire bathroom was a soggy, disgusting mess. I am unable to say how long it was in that state before I arrived and said something. Judging by the rest of my stay, it was more than likely a considerable stretch of time. (I eventually had to request a different roommate. Mine began threatening to stalk me on Facebook, I believe.)

I called my mother as soon as I could and gave her a glowing report. Something along the lines of, "Everything is great, everyone is being so nice, I'm doing great, I feel great. I slept really well, and I had an apple for breakfast; I think I'm ready to come home." *Translation: Get me out of here now.*

I remember being told the typical stay for patients was 3-5 days or so. I was there for almost 12.

For half of my stay, they continued my prescription of Celexa. Indeed. The thing that—unbeknownst to me until much later—was gradually launching me further and further into the unrelenting rabbit hole of mania, was being administered for at least 5 days after the start of the episode.

A bold strategy.

The nurses and techs were unkind. Well, most of them. There was one male nurse (or tech, I don't remember now) with a killer dry sense of humor that I dubbed "Never-Smiles Kyle". He was always kind, though a smile was rare for him (hence the nickname). And I believe there were some night nurses/technicians that weren't all bad. But most of the female personnel—especially if they were day staff—were condescending and hateful. I'll give you a few excerpts of things I remember:

I remember one of the nurses interviewing me about myself, my life, trying to get some personal background information I suppose … when she got to the question about what I had majored in, and I told her that I majored in Performing Arts with a concentration in Musical Theatre and planned on being an actor, she informed me that was not a real profession and chided me on my choice of direction in life. Nothing like being kicked when you're down, huh?

I remember being asked to participate in activities and often scolded when I didn't have the desire to do so, the staff even going so far as to threaten my visitation privileges. Once I was asked to sit down and do puzzles. I said, "Are all the pieces there?" The response? "I'm not sure." Then why on EARTH would I want to sit down and do an incomplete puzzle? I can't think of a worse activity to give to crazy people than a puzzle with missing pieces. Hello??

I remember Shirley. Shirley was the nastiest nurse of all at this particular hospital. There was one time I wanted to call my parents, and I asked Shirley if I could (I can't recall if I was required to ask, but I assume there were only certain times allotted for phone calls. Have to make a hospital feel as much like a prison as possible, you know?). She ignored me. She continued ignoring me and walked into the nurse's station that was blocked off and behind glass. I became inconsolable and began knocking on the glass trying to get her to answer me. She stood in there with other nurses, looking at me and laughing.

I've never hated someone so much since.

I later was informed through the psych-nurse-grapevine that Shirley had been fired at some point and possibly not terribly long after my stay there.

As well she should have been. She had no business working with psych patients. Frankly, most nurses in the psych profession have no business working with psych patients. The majority of those I've encountered on my own journey are brutally deficient in empathy.

I remember nurses trying to convince me my friend DJ was not real, that I was trying to call a figment of my imagination. After all, my parents had never heard of DJ, so he must not exist.

I don't remember all the drugs I was administered; I'd have to refer to my hospital records. I know about the continuation of the Celexa, but I don't remember everything else they tried.

Clearly nothing that worked.

My parents attempted repeatedly to speak directly to the doctor instead of playing telephone with nurses and technicians. They were told the doctor wouldn't speak to any family members.

Sure, why not? My health is clearly just fine in my own capable hands. (I have zero recall of my doctor's name or face if that helps paint a clear picture that I did not have the capacity to speak on my own behalf regarding my state of being. My mother even pulled up his professional photo online recently, and … nothing. I couldn't pick him out in a two-person lineup.)

When my parents kept bringing family members to visit, I was gradually having trouble recognizing them.

The hospital notes contain obvious insanity. I was apologizing for being a clone. I demanded an exorcism because I thought I was possessed. The news in the breakroom was making me paranoid. I was rarely sleeping.

Upon my final request (I tried daily) to the social worker that I be discharged, she defended the decision of holding me against my wishes by clarifying they thought the address listed on my intake report was an apartment, not that I lived with my mother.

Understandably.

I can see how sentence two of my admission report, "Patient lives with mom", could lead to confusion.

After 12 days, I was in a catastrophi-cally worse condition than when I arrived.

I left with a diagnosis of "Substance-Induced Psychotic Disorder," which the doctor decided had "resolved".

Evansville, IN

Guarantor: Jillian Weinzapfel V
Patient: Jillian Weinzapfel V

Jillian Weinzapfel V

Guarantor ID:

EVANSVILLE, IN

Visit Coverages:

This is not a bill. This is an itemization of your hospital services for:

| Patient: | Jillian Weinzapfel V | Admission Date: | 07/18/14 |
| Account: | | Discharge Date: | 07/29/14 |

Date	Rev Code	Procedure Code	Description	Qty	Amount
7/18/14	0637	63000003	OLANZAPINE ZYDIS 10 MG TBDP	1	
7/18/14				1	
7/18/14				1	
7/18/14				1	
7/19/14	0637	63000003	CITALOPRAM 40 MG TABS	1	
7/19/14				1	
7/19/14				1	
7/19/14				1	
7/19/14				1	
7/19/14				1	
7/19/14				1	
7/20/14				1	
7/20/14	0637	63000003	CITALOPRAM 40 MG TABS	1	
7/20/14	0250	J3486	ZIPRASIDONE 20 MG SOLR 1 EACH VIAL	2	
7/20/14	0637	63000003	OLANZAPINE ZYDIS 10 MG TBDP	1	
7/20/14				1	
7/21/14	0637	63000003	CITALOPRAM 40 MG TABS	1	
7/21/14				1	
7/22/14	0637	63000003	CITALOPRAM 40 MG TABS	1	
7/22/14	0637	63000003	ACETAMINOPHEN 325 MG TABS	2	
7/22/14	0637	63000003	ACETAMINOPHEN 325 MG TABS	1	
7/22/14				1	
7/23/14	0637	63000003	DIPHENHYDRAMINE 50 MG CAPS	1	
7/23/14	0637	63000003	CITALOPRAM 40 MG TABS	1	
7/23/14	0637	63000003	ARIPIPRAZOLE 2 MG TABS	1	
7/23/14	0637	63000003	ACETAMINOPHEN 325 MG TABS	1	
7/23/14				1	
7/24/14	0637	63000003	CITALOPRAM 20 MG TABS	1	
7/24/14	0637	63000003	ARIPIPRAZOLE 2 MG TABS	1	
7/24/14				1	
7/25/14	0637	63000003	CITALOPRAM 20 MG TABS	1	
7/25/14	0637	63000003	ARIPIPRAZOLE 5 MG TABS	1	
7/25/14				1	
7/26/14	0637	63000003	CITALOPRAM 20 MG TABS	1	
7/26/14	0637	63000003	ARIPIPRAZOLE 5 MG TABS	1	
7/26/14				1	

Guarantor: Jillian Weinzapfel V
Patient: Jillian Weinzapfel V

Date	Rev Code	Procedure Code	Description	Qty	Amount
7/27/14	0637	63000003	CITALOPRAM 20 MG TABS	1	
7/27/14				1	
7/27/14	0637	63000003	ARIPIPRAZOLE 5 MG TABS	1	
7/27/14				1	
7/28/14	0637	63000003	CITALOPRAM 20 MG TABS	1	
7/28/14	0637	63000003	ARIPIPRAZOLE 5 MG TABS	1	
7/28/14				1	
7/29/14	0637	63000003	CITALOPRAM 10 MG TABS	1	
				1	

*I found which drugs the hospital in Evansville
tried. Looks like we had a good time. Note
the continuation of the Citalopram (Celexa)
throughout the duration of my stay. (2014)*

Patient Name: Jillian V Weinzapfel   DOB: ████████   Duration of Service: 45 minutes
Discharge Type: Patient/family initiated   Condition on Discharge: Stable

DISCHARGE DIAGNOSES   *SIPD:*
THC abuse. SIPD which has resolved   "substance induced psychotic disorder"
████████████████

Past Medical History
Diagnosis   Date
• Unspecified psychosis **?**   7/21/2014

Medication List - SNAPSHOT

                                                  As of 7/29/2014 11:54 AM

START taking these medications
                                         Details

ARIPiprazole 5 MG tablet   Take 1 Tab (5 mg) by mouth at bedtime
Commonly known as: ABILIFY   for 30 days Indications: Psychosis/
                                         mood
                                         Quantity: 30 Tab
                                         Refills: 0

STOP taking these medications
                                         Stop taking
---
citalopram 40 MG tablet
Commonly known as: CELEXA

My discharge summary from the hospital
in Evansville. Certainly an interesting
and fairly vague conclusion. (2014)

BROOKE (MOTHER)

There's much to capture at this point in Jillian's recollection of her first episode of mania, psychosis, and hospitalization. Let me back up for just a second to Jillian's college experience, or at least my perspective of that time. Pursuing a degree in musical theatre is challenging. Not only did she have the usual classwork of a college degree, but add to that productions, private voice or dance lessons, and other community outreach. She was juggling a sometimes-overwhelming schedule and succeeding. We often had discussions regarding self-care – eating right, getting rest, etcetera – and I know she struggled with this area in relation to her degree pursuit, like many college students. She thought she needed medication, specifically mentioning depression medication. My read was different. We were both wrong.

When Jillian graduated and briefly returned home before her paid production in Virginia, she was definitely what I would call "up", particularly for her. In retrospect, this may have been a hypomanic phase. Hard to differentiate from her general excitement for her forthcoming theatrical venture. And when we (myself and her youngest siblings) visited her in Charlottesville, still she seemed happier and more positive relative to her seemingly-draining college days, but again I just attributed this to her finally being out in the theatrical world that she so loved. In addition to her energized demeanor, I do remember noticing some change in how she dressed, particularly the bandana in her hair that later became a telling sign. But again, this wasn't worrying. I mean, it was summer, and I was thrilled that she just seemed so happy.

When the Virginia gig ended and she returned to Indiana, she became the busy bee, readying a Facebook page and discussing other potential methods of pursuing her career. And then came the phone call from her father's medical office, a frantic drive, and all sorts of revelations and impossible decisions.

I didn't recognize my bright, intelligent, supremely verbal daughter. In place of coherent and clever conversation was this jumble of phrases and quickly alternating emotions, laughing and babbling followed by a rapid shift to profound distress that had her sobbing to her core. She kept referring to this DJ person, an unfamiliar name in the parade of classmates and castmates that I'd met or heard her mention. And what? She'd been taking an antidepressant? And smoking weed? When did this start? And then there was her overriding concern to apologize to her sister, Jenna, who came as summoned but had no idea what offense she had suffered in Jillian's mind. What was going on with my baby!?

And then a phone call from her brother, Josh, who also was at home for the summer. Apparently, DJ's attempt to help Jillian had resulted in a call to local Kentucky police who then contacted Indiana officers, and they were at the door to check on her welfare. Josh had no idea what to tell them as, in my rush to her side, there'd been no time to bring him up to speed. Just one domino after another, all crashing loudly in my head as I tried to catch up while my heart was just aching for my daughter.

Still sitting on the couch at the office, my mind races as I'm watching my daughter, consoling her, absorbing all this new information and considering what to do. As a responsible parent, you try to prepare for your role, right? But this isn't something I remember reading in any of those parenting books or magazines. And she's legally an adult, so even if I think we need to have her evaluated or tested, it's ultimately up to her. She could refuse.

We go to the local mental health facility to have her evaluated and, likely, admitted. She wanders around the waiting room, commenting on her hallucinations as she views the sterile pictures. I'm still uncertain that this isn't a result of "bad weed" – about this time there were horrifying social media posts regarding synthetic marijuana that stopped my heart – but I'm certain that we're at the right place to help sort this out, and she agreeably consents to be admitted. Neither of us have any idea how wrong we are – again.

The first indication I have that hospitalization might not be the answer occurs the first weekend. It was a Friday when she checked in, and we departed with assurances from the intake nurse that we would be able to communicate with Jillian the next day and visit her on Sunday, one of the two (or three?) allowed visitation days each week. Attempts to call her on Saturday are a maze of misunderstandings and incomplete instructions, and I'm distraught that I can't get through. And then Jillian calls me, early on Sunday morning, sounding bright and chipper and sharing that she has just enjoyed an apple for breakfast. Now I'm really worried. Because to this point in her young adult life, Jillian was rarely up early on a weekend morning, definitely not with a cheerful attitude, stopped eating breakfast regularly in high school, and **never** chose fruit for a snack (especially apples) despite all my best efforts ... much less for a meal and happy about it!

Now I'm on a mission to get into contact with someone to find out when I can visit and when I can speak with her doctor. Another phone maze, but I finally reach a nurse. While she was kind and helpful, I was left with more questions than answers, and a foreboding of what's to come. The nurse shares that the previous evening, they had to sedate Jillian because she was uncooperative, that today's promised visitation isn't in the cards and that – despite Jillian signing any and all authorizations to allow her medical team to share information with me and her father – her assigned physician doesn't talk with the family of patients ... at all ... for any reason. At this point, I feel my patience with this whole process begin to thin. For all her intelligence, my daughter obviously isn't capable of participating in her care at this time. Calmly, I ask the nurse at what point will they know when my daughter has returned to herself, her baseline personality, when they have no experience of her persona prior to this episode? And after describing that morning's phone call, detailing the inconsistencies with Jillian's normal mode, I add, "If you think that person is my daughter, you are quite mistaken."

Over the next couple of weeks, I'm there to visit with her every available chance, in addition to receiving usually urgent and mostly distraught phone calls from her almost daily. To each visit, she brings a notebook that the unit provided for group sessions. She brings it along to protect it from prying eyes of other patients, she explains.

As I look through the pages, my heart sinks. Jillian was in the habit of journaling from a young age. She loved to write. These scribblings bear no resemblance to her writing. There are no complete sentences. It looks like what a teenager would jot when bored in class, random words with no relation to a developed thought and in chaotic order, some sideways, as scattered as she now describes her internal thoughts in a manic state. Some visits I catch glimpses of my daughter, and she seems clearer, closing in on her baseline; other visits she seems to be devolving. When her siblings are along, they can sometimes interpret the phrases she uses as movie quotes or song lyrics that I just don't recognize and can at least provide some understanding of her expressions, but overall progress seems halted. While her mood is more stable than the day she was admitted, her words and thoughts are still jumbled and she now alternates between delusions and paranoia. She desperately wants to come home, but her discharge date keeps being pushed back, with staff threatening at times to take her to court to keep her in. The idea of this becoming public record scares me for her future, so I urge her to just cooperate, go along to get along, so that they will let her out. It's a powerless feeling that I won't soon forget or forgive.

It took nothing short of a miracle for them to release her, and – once they finally did – I was woefully unprepared for how to parent her in the state in which she now found herself.

And so, what normally might have been a lovely, relaxing summer took a dark turn for what I can only imagine Hell must feel like.

She's home. She's still not at all well, and I have no idea where we go from here, but she's home and out of that place that was leading her nowhere. First thing I think to do – besides grappling with getting her medication authorized and ordered (Why doesn't the hospital at least send her home with a starter pack if it's so critical?) – is to get some fresh air, take a walk together around "the Loop", an unofficial walking path around a local, hilly golf course ... something routine for us over the past couple of years when she's home from college. She's jittery, turning to look over her shoulder every couple of steps. Is this paranoia? Or is this real fear? She had mentioned on our visits a jealous roommate who had briefly been released and readmitted, letting Jillian know in menacing fashion that she found her on social media. Remembering several phone numbers collected in her notebooks from group sessions, I start to wonder whether her fear is justified. Who might have her phone number? Address? What might she have shared in her addled state? We turn around, head back to the car. We'll try again some other time. We need time to evaluate whether there's a real threat to our safety.

It's a strange time in our household. Of Jillian's younger five siblings, the youngest three are still in middle or high school, living at home, and it's summer break. The other two are college students, both working their summer jobs – one living at home, the other living off-campus in Evansville.

That isn't the strange part.

The first night home, Jillian turns on all the lights in the dead of night, waking her siblings and warning them of impending electrical fire, unplugging cords everywhere. Next day, her brother returns from work, and she insists that he is an impostor; he is NOT her brother, he doesn't smell right. She is not sleeping, busy instead decorating the dogs and anyone who walks through the door with jewelry. Another day, she tells me that today "Oliver" (I assume she's referring to a friend of hers from college – one I'd actually met) is in charge of her day and that she likes when he is in charge. She "hears" him (Looking back, most likely audio hallucinations – something most of us at that time were not aware could be a symptom of a manic episode with psychotic features. Certainly something most would attribute to schizophrenia, not bipolar disorder.). Not ever one for cooking, she starts making strange food concoctions ... thankfully nothing poisonous, but often not ingredients you would normally combine. Some of these she feeds to her beloved dog before I'm able to jump in and stop her.

As a condition of her discharge, we are required to follow up with an outpatient therapist, a licensed clinical social worker who was assigned by the hospital. At the first session, Amy invites me to sit in at the beginning to share my observations and insight into Jillian. She is calm and caring. Follow-up sessions are just the two of them. Jillian likes her so well that she tells me after a session one day that Amy must be her mother, not me. Frankly, I was happy for her to establish a connection, so I bit back any argument.

When we arrive home, the delusions make themselves ever more apparent when Jillian asks,

"When were you going to tell me?"

I'm lost.

"Tell you what?"

"That Jonah and Jourdan (her youngest siblings) are mine?"

"Your ... children?"

"Yes."

I'm looking for the punch line. Her jaw is set; she truly believes this is the relationship. Gently, I try to explain that they are her siblings. She doesn't seem to buy it, but she drops the conversation. Maybe somewhere deep down, she recognizes this? We are still going nowhere on this journey.

((Hi, it's me. A quick interruption here. Though I have no recollection of this conversation, much less the entirety of what my mother is recounting through this brief, though I'm sure seemingly-eternal, interim period between hospitals ... and it's *extremely* humiliating to see in print ... I think that—firstly, it's important to ig-nore my reflexive desire to delete it. I intend to include it instead, in order to show how starkly debilitated psychosis can render someone's capacity to recognize unobjectionable reality and things they've long-accepted as indisputable facts. And secondly, I wanted to jump in and say this was not the lone occasion of psychosis when I was utterly sure I had children. I have no idea who it is I become when manic with psychotic features, but it's

very intriguing to me to see how it almost sort of crosses over into DID, Dis-
sociative Identity Disorder. I don't say
this with much clinical knowledge of DID;
I merely find it fascinating that part of
who I "become" when manic seems to have a
consistent trait of thinking I have children, and always 2 of them. Anywho. Some
things I wanted to highlight. I'll shut up
now. Carry on.))

At this point, I've taken her car keys, worrying not just that she might cause an accident, but also that she might drive off and not be able to find her way home. She needs constant supervision, and other family chip in at times, but most of this duty falls to me and her younger siblings.

Her sister and older brother's then-girlfriend take her to the mall. They describe convincing her to return items to the shelves that she has stuffed into her bag.

She's in constant motion.

A neighbor across the pond (a literal pond, not refer-ring to someone in Europe) finds her pouring gasoline on a small pile of brush and lighting a fire. This isn't the first fire she has recently lit, sometimes lighting our brush pile in the night.

Time to hide the matches and lighters.

One evening, she hitchhikes to a local bar. I can't quite remember how I learned about this, but I can remember she reported her adventure without a hint of guile.

((Hi, sorry, me again. Wonder of wonder,
miracle of miracles (as it's put in *Fid-
dler on the Roof*), I actually know **exactly**

how she found out because I somehow have
recall on a goodly portion of this event.
I couldn't even begin to tell you how I
remember, but I know I walked to a public
building not far from our house—very late
at night—and approached a man and a woman
talking in the parking lot. I'm not sure
how I finagled it (I'm sure I seemed piti-
able enough), but I essentially told the
man that I needed a ride, and he obliged
and thankfully did not feel the urge to
just, you know, murder me. I don't have any
recall of this man, but shoutout to him
for being a real trooper and not leaving
me in some ditch. I asked him to drop me
at the bar, where I met a young man, about
my age (give or take a year or two) named
Nick. (Yes, that is his real name. Yes, I
actually somehow 100% remember exactly who
this person is, even though I'd never met
him previously and have never interacted
with him since. Again, I can't even begin
to tell you how I could possibly retain
this information.) So Nick and I began
flirting, and he invited me to shoot some
rounds of pool with him and his friends.
I told him, "I don't really know how to
play," but I was absolutely lying. It's how
I spent a major chunk of my downtime in
Charlottesville when not performing. The
cast and crew members were living in frat
houses just a short walk from the theatre,
which were all equipped with pool tables,

though one of the tables was super janky and had a horrible lean, so you had to kind of account for that before you took a turn … you're right. Irrelevant. Okay, so I was hustling this guy. I knew how to play pool and had even been very recently sharpening my skills. He must've been quite drunk to be hustled by someone in my condition. Sadly hilarious, sorry, Nick. We were flirting, he was buying me drinks (Ah, yes, alcohol will help), there was even possible kissing? That, I don't remember. But I think it's highly probable because suddenly I invited him back to my place. Well … my mom's place. (There are many horror stories of bipolar people engaging in promiscuity. I wasn't exactly a prude at this juncture in my young adult life, but I wasn't known to sleep with total strangers, either.) I remembered at some point (hopefully can't have been too long) that I didn't have a car, and really there was no way either of us could drive anyway. I told him we could walk. A couple of fun little tidbits here: 1. My mom's house is not really anywhere close to this bar. Sure, it's only a 10- to 15-minute drive tops, but it's a forever-long walk. If we'd actually walked to my mother's house from the bar, it's unlikely we would've reached it until sometime the following morning, and 2. I don't quite remember how to get there. He redirected the walk to another nearby bar, and I called my mom to tell her … this is where it's fuzzy … to tell her I don't know where I am? To tell her I need to be picked up? Not sure. But I know she had to come get me. So I left Nick and went home with my fuming and exhausted mother. And that must've been the *weirdest* one-off night of Nick's life that he probably doesn't have any recollection of. Good. Times.))

She's been dressing provocatively, cut off jean shorts become her new favorite, not her usual sweatpants.

Now I take her phone as well – trying to protect her from herself – and my sister and I begin discussing options for help in Indianapolis. The kids will be returning to school soon, and their sports and other activities will be kicking up, and – even though my work summers are slow – tax season is fast approaching, and there's no way I can keep up with her wandering days and sleepless nights with a full daily schedule and no "watchers" at home.

She breaks down one evening about her lack of sleep. She just feels so tired, if only she could rest. My heart hurts for my forlorn daughter.

While her siblings are away one weekend at their father's, I consult with her former pediatrician – a longtime friend – and try to bring about conditions to assist her with sleep; lowering the lights and quieting the environment are much easier to do with an empty house. She takes some Benadryl and is drowsy enough to agree to slip into bed in the cool and quiet basement. Maybe, just maybe … ?

Aaaannnnnddddd, she's back. In rip-roaring fashion, all the lights turned on, frantically dancing in front of the mirrored, sliding-glass doors, turning and twisting, jumping and spinning. It dawns on me: She's fighting to stay awake!

And now she's crying, exhausted from her exhortations, perhaps even a little frustrated with the failure, and she confirms my suspicion. She doesn't want to sleep, she admits, because then she'll have "the nightmares," scary images that fuel her despair. With these garbled admissions, I realize we've got to find some help. The next day, I call the help line for the Indianapolis hospital. It's been nearly a month – Has it really only been that long? Feels like a lifetime – since that fateful day, we are both exhausted, and we are still getting nowhere.

JONAH & JOURDAN
(YOUNGEST BROTHER AND SISTER, RESPECTIVELY)

Oh, hello.

My name is Jonah. I am the sixth child out of seven, and I was a 13-year-old living at home at the time in question. Unlike the other authors in this book, my recollection of the events is crystal clear, so I suggest taking everything I write as a fact.

Jillian and I have always had a special kind of relationship. She discovered my comedic potential, taught me how to do long division, and she was once mistaken to be my mother after I was almost backed over in a Walmart parking lot. Because she was on the phone, a bystander scolded her to watch her child. That's right, not all of Jillian's manic delusions were entirely misguided. In fact, you'll see that Jourdan and I don't think she gives herself enough credit. She did raise me, in a way, much how I raised our next guest and my co-author. Say hi to the folks, Jourdan!

Hi to the folks, Jourdan! Ahaha classic. Hi folks, and welcome to your new favorite chapter in the book. I'm Jourdan, the 7th-born and youngest of the siblings, still getting called the "baby of the family," at 20 years old. Jillian is my eldest sister, and for as long as I can remember, the main trait tying together my concept of "Jillian" is that she does what she pleases.

Jillian is stubborn and independent ...

Such a Taurus.

((Jillian, here. Firstly, you know nothing about astrology, so you hush with your, "SuCh A tAuRuS." Secondly, it's Jourdan's turn to talk, so ... you hush even MORE. Carry on, Jourdan.))

... ... and she was considered the trailblazer when it came to the rules in our family. By that, I mean she completely ignored them, and she inspired the introduction of many more. I thought Jillian was very cool (with her digital cameras, dance/vocal talents, THE most 2000s jeans, etc.) and also terrifying. This was due to a few facts: (1) She followed me with a knife saying, "I'm not the real Jillian," as a prank when I was 5 (~15 y/o Jillian for perspective)...

((IT WAS A JOKE. Albeit a poor one. But at the time? Hilarious. What can I say? 15-year-olds are stupid; we all know this.))

... and (2) I was a complete goody-two-shoes, so her lack of fear for authority was, frankly, enough to make me cry thinking about at that age. Seeing as I was only eleven when Jillian came home from Virginia that erratic 2014 summer, I do remember bits and pieces, but certain ones are missing, such as initially finding out about Jillian's first hospital admission. For whatever strange reasons, Jonah's slightly-less-adolescent, 13 y/o brain has full recollection, so here you fucking go.

My testimonial begins with the Saturday that Jillian was first taken to the Evansville hospital. I remember vividly that I had gotten into trouble for something at our dad's house, and I had a group date at the movie theater that evening that I *could not* miss. After pouting in my room for some time because Dad wouldn't let me go, he trudged up the stairs to share the dreadful news: Jillian had to be hospitalized for smoking too much weed. And I bawled my eyes out. As my mother previously mentioned, I too had heard of the dangers of synthetic marijuana in my sixth-grade health class, where they made it seem super common. I was terrified.

I ended up getting to go to the movies, but I remember deciding that I was going to sulk the entire evening (Then again, did I get my first kiss that night?). Jourdan and I never got the opportunity to visit her in the hospital, but our first encounter with Jillian was memorable, nonetheless. She, my mother, Jules, Jourdan, and I went to pick up dinner at Subway on her first night home. Jillian was looking around a bunch as if she was being watched, and I remember thinking that the guy on the veggie side of the counter was flirting with her, which probably scared her more than anything else (Sorry, guy). It was later that night we heard about Brandon/Brandy, her ex-roommate and stalker from the hospital …

The lights came on in our room that September school night extremely late, and Jillian was telling me (a) Merry Christmas (?) and (b) {As I remember it} Brandy was going to blow up our house by hacking into its electrical items, so we had to unplug everything in the house stat. Obviously, I rushed to help my sister save the day because I was scared as shit. I participated in practically all Jillian's antics, i.e. the cooking of Gordon Ramsay's dreams, revolutionary dog fashion, etc., eventually causing my mom to frustratedly ask, "Why do you listen to her?" to which I promptly responded, "I'm eleven."

Now, as far as our cooking goes, I only ever helped on one occasion when I had the free time necessary to dedicate to such projects; I'd seen her commit to many of these in that kitchen at this point. My sister was finally back home (After disappearing in my eyes when in the hospital due to the lesser details my parents thought I could handle), and I was excited to participate in, and bond through, her new hobby. So, when she told me that we were just going to find EVERYTHING sweet in that whole fucking kitchen and put it in one bowl and just stir and microwave, I. was. stoked. Maple syrup, Hershey's chocolate, chocolate chips, marshmallows, chocolate milk?, honey, vanilla extract, cinnamon, sugar, butter, graham crackers, you name it, we got it. On record, we did NOT feed this specific one to Kirby; no gremlins were harmed in the making of my masterpiece. Let's just say: Mom was not too proud of her little chefs' clean-up job ... haha oops.

BUT this just brings us back to Jillian not giving herself enough credit: She totally had a genius phase! Her cooking could bring God himself both to his knees and to tears with sheer delight and possibly diabetes (But he's God; he can take care of that).

It may sound as though we are completely disregarding Jillian's "no joking" rule, and maybe we are, but our tiny, pre-teen brains did not comprehend the severity of the situation at hand. Thus, our then naïveté about the world and about the enigmatic nature of mental illness that still perplexes scientists today, led to some pretty hilarious misconceptions. Despite our jovial tone about this first episode, there was a genuine fear that we would never get back the sister we once recognized and felt truly recognized us back (and not as her children). We missed her.

JENNA
(YOUNGER SISTER/PSYCH NURSE)

The first time I watched my older sister's brain break before my eyes was the most terrifying and impactful event of my life thus far.

Just to give a little backstory on myself (to better show my state of mind), I was in the beginning stages of nursing school at the time and under a fair amount of stress ... to put it lightly. I was in class every single weekday from 8 AM to 3-4 PM. When I wasn't studying, I was working at the hospital as a patient care tech in the intensive care unit for neonates or on the pediatric ward, anywhere from 3 PM to 7 AM (whatever part of those shifts was available). In all my free time (ha-ha), I would squeeze in cheering for the college I was attending, as well as part-time-assistant-coaching gymnastics for a former coach of mine. So, I didn't spend nearly enough time with my family as a result (which some of them often reminded me, rightfully so).

I remember getting a call from my father very early in the morning. Mind you, had I not been in Nursing School Mode (which does not pause during the summer) and on this sleep schedule, I would NOT be awake at this time of day, and my family would absolutely know this and not even attempt to call. But I got a call from him, which was already weird. Not only was he calling in the early morning hours, but a phone call as opposed to his usual text message? It made me nervous, so I answered immediately. He tells me that Jillian is at his office (also weird, as their relationship has never exactly been peachy), and she is concerned with the state of things between her and me. She is hysterical and believes we are in a huge fight and wants to make it right. It almost seems as if she believes something terrible is going to happen, like she doesn't want it "to end" with us in this state.

I am utterly confused. We had plenty of fights when we were sharing a bedroom as adolescents, don't get me wrong, but in the more recent years? I couldn't even recall the last time we had spoken, much less fought about something. We were much more distant nowadays; when we did get to see and talk to each other, there was no fighting. We weren't constantly in each other's area. More specifically, I wasn't constantly making her space look like a tornado had moved through the room or borrowing her clothes or accessories without asking and ruining them. We had no real reason to fight anymore and just enough time to see each other, catch up, and continue living our lives.

The urgency in Dad's voice with his, "I think you better get down here," on the phone, the fact that he and Mom were trying to figure out what was going on together, like, *in the same place*, the fact

83

that Jillian actually turned up at his office for help (again, so weird), and the fact that it was one of my siblings, period, was enough to send a chill right to my spine and dread deep into the pit of my stomach. Something is severely wrong with this picture. So, I go to my father's office to meet with him, my mother, and my sister.

When I arrive, Jillian is on the couch and absolutely out of her mind, loopy like I had never witnessed anyone before. She is euphoric one moment, tearful the next, with a disorganized thought-process-whirlwind that doesn't stop ... but at the same time, she looks so exhausted. She began to talk about this fight she seemed to believe we had while I tried to convince her we were fine and that I did not recall any fight, but even if there was one, not to worry about it.

This was my first encounter with psychosis.

And one that I have somewhat blocked out, due to the fact that it was someone I look up to and love with all my heart. Not because it changes that I look up to her or love her; because, if anything, watching how resilient and strong she had to be through all this has made that only grow. But if you—as the reader—have watched a loved one go through anything traumatic, especially something that causes them to completely lose a sense of self such as mental illness or brain trauma, it hurts you deep into your soul. Especially since at this point, we don't even know WHAT this is, IF it can be resolved, WHEN it will be resolved, everything is up in the air.

And feeling completely helpless in your ability to do anything for them shatters you to the core.

My parents ultimately decided to take her to a facility in our hometown. By some miracle, she signed herself in voluntarily. As she was an adult, she had to make the choice to receive care, but I did not think (especially given her current state of mind) there was any way she would. I believe I was only able to visit once while she was there. She brought down some coloring pages she made and showed a little improvement ... but to be totally honest, it did not seem that she had made much. During that short visit, which—if I remember correctly—was closer to the end of her stay than the beginning, I recall her speaking about, "Receiving the messages meant for her," from the TV program on in the unit.

When she was released, we still had to keep a very watchful eye on her because the hospital had essentially failed her in the end. She was still very much disorganized, grandiose, etc. and left with a vague and "resolved" diagnosis and medications that didn't seem to be doing much of anything. She was making strange food concoctions, dressing up the dogs in capes and plastic jewelry, and remained in a bubbly, euphoric state that was just not the older sister I was accustomed to.

So, a side note on how they failed her:

I did not know this at the time because I was not yet in the position I am now. I am now an experienced psych nurse of 5.5 years, who is utterly shocked at the way the doctor went about her care.

At the time, I thought she had gotten ahold of K2 because she was smoking marijuana, and I thought maybe someone duped her with some synthetic crap. I also knew she had taken slightly more of her Celexa than she was supposed to and was unaware that one capsule more than usual would throw her into a full-blown episode; although, in addition to the marijuana and the stress she was under, I suppose it makes sense. My then-uneducated guesses aside, the *very educated* psychiatrist in charge of her care decided to CONTINUE the very medication that she took to induce her current episode and ADD to the serotonin that was already storming her brain.

Working in a very similar psychiatric facility now, it is common sense that we **never** restart medication that someone has overdosed on, no matter if they took 2 or 30 of the pill, due to the fact that they have an abundance of it in their system already. One would think, even with very little knowledge, the first step after taking too much of a medication is to immediately stop taking said medication to give the body a chance to rid itself of the overload. THAT one simple thing could have changed a lot of the outcome of this situation, and it is something that irks me to this day.

Unfortunately, as is the case in most of America, there is simply a lack of resources when it comes to adequate mental healthcare. Especially on a local level in Southern Indiana, options are so limited for acute crisis (e.g. patients with homicidal/ suicidal ideation, needing rehab, or experiencing psychosis) care; there are about 3 places you can go specifically for mental health, and **none** of them provide 'medical care,' so you must be medically cleared. In other words, if you were to go to the ER and would need extra assistance in the way of issues needing IV medication, continuous oxygen, cardiac monitoring, PT/OT consults (help with activities of daily living like showering, toileting, etc. due to physical incapabilities), STAT labs that need repeated often and in a timely manner, illnesses that require certain types of isolation, etc., the psych facility would not accept you because it isn't equipped to provide that type of care. Even for outpatient care: It can take months to get into an outpatient provider, and by the time you *do* get an appointment, you are in crisis and probably need more than they can provide with outpatient treatment. Additionally, as far as acute care, the facility that Jillian went to is one of the ONLY facilities in town that will take "Emergency Detention" patients (i.e. patients that have been court-ordered by a judge to be held for 72 business hours). These are the patients that are deemed a harm to themselves (or others) or gravely disabled that do not wish to seek help but are forced to by law. These people are usually angry, and therefore violent, due to feeling their rights have been violated. I believe this same facility also takes over 90% of CIT (Crisis Intervention Team) patients. These are people the police bring into the ER from the community, due to receiving calls from concerned citizens and determining there is mental health involved.

Resources are spread THIN. There are not enough:

1.   Facilities, period.

2.   People willing to work in mental health to run said facilities.

3.   People with the *right mentality* to run or work the facilities.

4.   Financial funds with which to obtain the right resources that provide adequate care in said facilities.

5.   Financial funds with which to provide adequate research into mental health as a whole.

6.   I mean the list goes on and on and on.

7.   And on.

Okay, off my soap box. For now.

CHAPTER FIVE

As luck would have it, that was not my worst hospital stay. To be fair, it's difficult to rank them. All four were terrible, each in its own way.

Wait, four hospitalizations? I thought you had two manic episodes …?

Yes. Four hospitalizations in three different hospitals between two manic episodes, all in one crazy.

Why? How?

I'll get there.

The first hospitalization resulted in a fairly vague diagnosis of unspecified psychosis (substance-induced) that the doctor claimed had "resolved." That was in Evansville, Indiana (the city I grew up in). The "pickin's" are slim for mental healthcare in Evansville, so after I was discharged and in a DECIDEDLY WORSE condition from the first hospital (*Resolved indeed)*, my mother opted to look elsewhere. She turned to Indianapolis.

Talk about the worst sleepaway summer camp of my life.

To the Evansville hospital's credit, we were allowed to walk around outside a little. The courtyard was *tiny*, but still. The sun and fresh air were much needed. In fact, all three other hospital stays (two at the same hospital in California) allowed for outside recreational time.

Indianapolis was a prison. For three-ish weeks.

I thought 11 days was an eternity. Do you think I was prepared for 3 weeks? With no sunshine or fresh air? In worse condition than when the episode began back in mid-July?

Reader, I assure you, I was absolutely not.

Intake is a distant blur. I was incoherent. Given that I was stuck in a manic episode (and had been for weeks) with no end in sight, this doesn't surprise me. I left the Evansville hospital with a sort-of-fuzzy diagnosis, one that the doctor himself noted was apparently not an ongoing issue. If you don't understand the significance of this, allow me to shed a little light.

If someone leaves a hospital with a "resolved," vaguely concerning diagnosis, what is the treatment plan?

Precisely. It's a best-guess kind of scenario.

If I remember correctly, they had me on Abilify (Aripiprazole—an antipsychotic) upon my release. It had me screaming in the car one day because I felt like my blood was frozen in my veins and panicked.

As a result of not receiving a proper diagnosis or treatment plan, I was substantially more unintelligible by the time I arrived in Indianapolis. My mom drove (Obviously … could you imagine??), and we met my older brother and my aunt (her sister) who lived in or near Indy, respectively. Those three have a much better sense of what happened during intake than I do.

I know I seemed insane enough to be there. For 3 weeks.

And my doctor? Hated me. Dr. S _ _ _ . Her, I remember. She was not a fan. I was merely trying to get out as soon as possible, and she was having NONE of it. And no matter how I approached her—if I was kind, if I was hysterical, if I had questions, if I had nothing to say—she seemed to me to be unkind, unhelpful, and unsympathetic. Always just cold and clinical.

I was put on every antipsychotic known to man.

That's a lie.

But I was put on a plethora of antipsychotics. They figured they'd try anything. For all intents and purposes, it was as though they were chucking figurative darts at a dartboard. As a direct result, this hospital stay is hazier. Not terribly shocking, considering the state my brain must've been in.

Hyperactive, angry, confused mush.

I remember only a handful of truly traumatizing things. I'm sure the rest of it is buried in my psyche somewhere, waiting to be unleashed at inopportune moments, as it goes with Post-Traumatic Stress Disorder. The fragments I remember are as follows:

Once, an elderly gentleman (a patient, of course) decided to stand in the doorway of his room and masturbate where everyone could see him until someone finally had to tell him to close the door, which was a process. There was a bit of a back-and-forth (*Ba-Dum-Tss*. Get it? A back-and-forth? Gross, I'm sorry. I'll see myself out.) before the staff member finally had to close it. He was an older gentleman, but I'm 99% certain he knew exactly what he was doing. There was too much eye contact happening (I assure you, NOT with me) for him to be unaware.

An enormously tall gentleman named Mark (also a patient) who let me know, repeatedly, that he liked "white women" and once busted into my room at 3 in the morning telling me we were "getting out of here."

Being strapped down to a table and stripped down by at least three nurses and stuck with a needle of who-knows-what in my inner thigh because I wouldn't (probably couldn't) sleep.

Being locked alone in a room the size of a closet with meditation music playing on blast because it was evidently supposed to "calm me down," when I was feeling severely agitated. What reason did I have to be so worked up, I wonder?

A high school friend of mine visiting to ask if I would be a bridesmaid in her wedding. (I promise you, even if you think you understand how humiliating this was, you cannot fathom. We haven't really spoken since her wedding.)

That's … about it. I recall that it was a bigger facility, and I was moved around several times. Most of the nurses and technicians were far kinder here than they had been in Evansville.

But three weeks is a long time to be stuck inside and administered antipsychotics that aren't helping.

Eventually, I don't remember much leading up to it, but I know I began refusing to swallow whatever pills I was being prescribed. As my release date was approaching, Dr. S _ _ _ decided to court order me.

Yes, I went to court. While manic. On anti-psychotics. I had to try and defend myself in this state.

It's truly a blessing that I don't remember much.

This was the first time, according to my aunt and mother, that the term "Schizophrenia" was used to describe what was happening to me.

IN COURT.

Not surprising, then, that I lost. Schizophrenia would give any judge the impression that I was a danger to—not only myself—but everyone else. I had to resume taking the medications being tossed at my gullet, and my stay was changed over from "Voluntary" to "Involuntary" I believe, thereby extending the duration until my eventual release.

I did learn a very important lesson from taking the never-ending stream of various antipsychotics, though.

No matter how many antipsychotics I am prescribed, none of them will be able to bring me back to my baseline. Not really. They will break the psychosis and *me*—numbing me into a person I don't recognize—but they won't get to the root of the issue, not without the aid of a mood stabilizer. So far as I know, anyway.

I left with an incorrect diagnosis of Undifferentiated Schizophrenia (A diagnosis—by the way—that is no longer in use by the medical community.). And I was a shell of a human. For a long while.

See, not always so easy to laugh about.

STATE OF INDIANA)
) SS:
COUNTY OF ████)

IN THE ████ SUPERIOR COURT
PROBATE DIVISION ████ JUDGE

████ STRESS CENTER
    Petitioner

CAUSE NUMBER: ████

JILLIAN WEINZAPFEL
    Respondent

IN THE MATTER OF THE COMMITMENT OF:

JILLIAN WEINZAPFEL

FILED

AUG 26 2014

Judge of the
████ County Court
Probate Division

ORDER SETTING COMMITMENT HEARING AND DIRECTING RESPONDENT TO APPEAR

A Petition for Involuntary Commitment with a Physician's Statement attached was filed by ████ S██, MD on **August 25, 2014.**

An evidentiary hearing is set for **September 3, 2014, at 8:15 o'clock a.m.** in the ████ SUPERIOR COURT ● - PROBATE DIVISION ████ BUILDING.
The hearing shall determine if Respondent is mentally ill and dangerous or is mentally ill and gravely disabled (as those terms are defined in IC 12-7-2) and if so, to which facility Respondent shall be committed.

The respondent **JILLIAN WEINZAPFEL** is ordered to appear at the hearing unless his attorney appears on his behalf instead.

The Court appoints ████ to serve as counsel for the Respondent unless Respondent retains other counsel or validly waives the right to be represented by counsel. Counsel's office address and telephone are: ████ Street, Suite ██, Indianapolis, IN██ Phone ████ OR ████ IS THE COURT APPOINTED ATTORNEY FOR THE RESPONDENT WHICH GIVES ████ FULL ACCESS TO THIS PATIENT AND RECORDS WHICH PERTAIN TO THIS PATIENT.

(OPTIONAL) The Court appoints   M.D. to examine Respondent and to submit a Physician's Statement to the Court prior to the hearing. Respondent is directed to schedule an appointment with said physician and to appear at said physician's office at the scheduled time.

The Sheriff is directed to serve a Summons together with a copy of the Petition, the Physician's Statement (s), the Notice of Rights and Procedures, and this Order upon Respondent at   not less than two (2) days (excluding Saturdays, Sundays and legal holidays) prior to the hearing.

The Clerk is directed to mail a copy of this Order and the Notice of Rights and procedures to the Petitioner (s), the Physician (s) who signed Statements, counsel for the parties, and the following additional persons: .

SO ORDERED this 26TH day of August, 2014.

████
Judge
Superior Court - Probate Division

My court summons from my time at the Indianapolis hospital. (2014)

STATE OF INDIANA)
) SS:
COUNTY OF ███████)

IN THE ███████ COUNTY SUPERIOR
COURT ROOM NO. ●
CAUSE NO. _____

IN THE MATTER OF THE COMMITMENT OF)
)
Lillian Weinzapfel   )
)
████████ Stress Center   )
)
Indianapolis, IN ████████   )
)
                    Petitioner,   )
)
            and   )
)
Lillian Weinzapfel   )
)
                    Respondent,   )

PHYSICIAN'S STATEMENT

1. I, ██████████████████, M.D., the undersigned physician,

   X hold a valid license to practice medicine in Indiana, issued by the Medical
      Licensing Board of Indiana, or
   ___ am a medical officer of the United States Government who is in Indiana
      performing official duties.

2. On the 24 day of August, 20__, within the past thirty (30) days, I examined
   Respondent, Lillian Weinzapfel, the person whose commitment is
   sought.

3. In my professional opinion, this person is suffering from:
   X a psychiatric disorder

   ___ a developmental disability (examples: retardation, epilepsy)

   ___ alcoholism/addiction to narcotics or dangerous substances, or

   ___ other _____

   which substantially disturbs Respondent's thinking, feelings, or behavior, and impairs
   Respondent's ability to function. Specifically:
   Delusional thoughts - Disorganized
   thoughts

*The physician's statement for
the court summons. (2014)*

7. In my professional opinion, each of the following facilities is suitable for the necessary care, treatment, and protection of Respondent and others:

_____ _Three Center_

Of these, the one(s) with the least restrictive environment is (are):

_____

8. In my opinion, the type of commitment that would be sufficient to achieve improvement in the Respondent's condition is:

X Temporary (not to exceed ninety days).
___ Regular (indefinite, but to be review by the Court annually).

9. If commitment is ordered, Respondent should be required to comply with the following special conditions in order to achieve improvement in the Respondent's condition:

a. That Respondent take all medication(s) as prescribed.
b. That Respondent attend all clinic sessions as scheduled.
c. That Respondent maintain h⌐✓ address and telephone number, on record, if and when Respondent is placed on outpatient commitment.
d. That Respondent no harass or assault family members or others.
e. That Respondent not use alcohol or drugs, other than those prescribed by a certified medical doctor.
f. _____
g. _____

10. In my opinion, holding the hearing in the courtroom would have a harmful effect on the Respondent's health or well being.

___ Yes   X No

Dated: _8/24/14_   Physician's Signature: _____

Physician Name (print): ▉▉▉▉▉▉▉▉

Address: ▉▉▉▉▉▉
Indianapolis, IN ▉▉▉

Telephone: ▉▉▉▉

The physician's statement for the court summons. (2014)

(COMPLETE 4a and/or 4b. COMPLETE BOTH ONLY IF BOTH ARE APPLICABLE.)

4a. In my professional opinion, Respondent is dangerous in that, as a result of the condition(s) specified in Paragraph 3, Respondent presents a substantial risk of harm to (___) self, or (___) others. Specifically:

_____

_____

4b. In my professional opinion, Respondent is gravely disabled in that, as a result of the condition(s) specified in Paragraph 3, Respondent is in danger of coming to harm because of

_____ an inability to provide for food, clothing, shelter, or other essential human needs, or

__X__ a substantial impairment or obvious deterioration in judgment, reasoning, or behavior that results in Respondent's inability to function independently.

Specifically: Delusional - significantly

impaired judgment

Does the Respondent have family, friends, or others willing and able to assist in meeting those needs? (___) Yes (X) No

5. In my professional opinion:

__X__ This person is in need of custody, care, or treatment in an appropriate facility.

_____ Outpatient treatment would be adequate.

_____ Commitment would not be necessary if this person were taking medication.

_____ This person can be relied upon to take medication as prescribed.

_____ There are family members or friends willing and able to see to it that this person takes medication as prescribed.

_____ Commitment would not be necessary if a legal guardian were appointed for this person.

6. I have discussed with the Respondent the advisability of obtaining treatment on a voluntary basis, and Respondent:

_____ has refused to begin voluntary treatment; or

__X__ is not an appropriate person for voluntary treatment because: delusional thinking - impaired judgment

_____ Respondent is not competent, at this time, to agree.

The physician's statement for the court summons. (2014)

98

Jillian Vanessa Weinzapfel
September 4, 2014
2:45 pm

Exhausted

I'm supposed to take 10 minutes and write about the word "exhausted." Which -- actually -- seems exhausting in and of itself. It's much like writing a timed essay. Running in a circle for 10 minutes is exhausting. Writing for 10 minutes is hand cramp central. Why would anyone take the time? The answer is clearly no one would.

This is redundant to say the least. Even the music sucks. I won't be able to share this shit with anyone. That's what this is. Straight up garbage.

10 minutes??? Seriously. WHY. I mean, I could write for 20, but that doesn't mean I WANT to. Or HAVE to. Groups are silly. We're all adults here. Why don't we just sit around and swap stories or tell jokes? Might as well.

When I found this writing from a group, I was shocked. Not only did I not know it existed (of course), it's unexpectedly coherent for being merely a day after my appearance in court. (2014)

JACOB (OLDER BROTHER)

BEING JILLIAN'S ONLY OLDER SIBLING HAS NEVER BEEN A WALK IN THE PARK, PER SE. NOT ONLY ARE WE EACH THE OLDEST SIBLING OF OUR GENDER (ME, BEING THE OLDEST BOY/HER, THE OLDEST GIRL), WHICH LED TO A GREAT DEAL OF CLASHING AS WE WERE GROWING UP, BUT OUR PERSONALITIES ARE **COMPLETE** OPPOSITES. IN EVERY WAY. WHEREAS I WAS ALWAYS QUIETER AND MORE RESERVED, SHE WAS MORE RAMBUNCTIOUS AND FREE-SPIRITED. WHERE I AM MORE LOGICALLY DRIVEN AND LEFT-BRAINED, SHE SEEMED MORE DRIVEN BY EMOTION AND HER THOUGHT PATTERNS LEANED MORE RIGHT-BRAINED. I WAS THE RULE-FOLLOWER, THE POSTER OLDEST CHILD; SHE WAS CONSTANTLY PUSHING HER BOUNDARIES, QUESTIONING AUTHORITY, AND MOST OF THE TIME JUST FLAT BREAKING THE RULES. I CAN'T REMEMBER BEING GROUNDED TOO MUCH; SHE WAS GROUNDED HER ENTIRE 7TH-GRADE YEAR. I WAS ALWAYS MORE SERIOUS; HER CHILDHOOD NICKNAME WAS "SILLY JILLI".

NOT THAT I ALWAYS MINDED BEING TOTAL OP-POSITES. AFTER ALL, AS HER DUTIFUL OLDER BROTHER, I CATERED TO HER BEFORE SHE EVEN LEARNED TO WALK. IF SHE POINTED AT ANY OBJECT

IN THE ROOM, I'D GO AND GET IT FOR HER (THIS RESULTED IN HER BEING THE SLOWEST TO LEARN TO WALK ... WHOOPS.). WHEN WE GOT TO BE A LITTLE OLDER, I'D PICK A DIFFERENT SEAT WHEN SHE WOULD INSIST HER IMAGINARY FRIEND WAS SITTING WHERE I TRIED TO. SHE WAS MY GO-TO SCENE PARTNER TO ENDLESSLY QUOTE FROM *THE LION KING* WHILE IN THE CAR. WE HAD THE ENTIRE MOVIE MEMORIZED, WHICH MOM LOVED. BUT ... THE CLASHING.

FROM GETTING MY FIRST ROUND OF STITCHES WHEN SHE HIT ME WITH A GOLF CLUB (A DRIVER, TO BE PRECISE. P.S. JILLIAN, "LOOK AT ALL THE BLOOD!" WAS A BIG HELP WHILE I WAS GETTING MY STITCHES. FOR THE FIRST TIME. SO THANKS FOR THAT.) ... .

((Time Out! Okay, not my proudest childhood moment, but I do want to clarify that he was hit on the BACKSWING. It was not totally intentional. I'm not absolving myself, but I want to make it absolutely clear I didn't have a penchant for violence. At least, not all the time.))

... TO POWER STRUGGLES WHEN I WAS LEFT IN CHARGE AT HOME, TO GETTING INTO STUPID (SOMETIMES VIOLENT, E.G. BITING, PUNCHING, YOU NAME IT) ARGUMENTS ON THE WAY TO SCHOOL, THE LIST COULD GO ON AND ON. ETC., ETC., ETC.

PERHAPS WE DIDN'T ALWAYS GET ALONG, BUT I NEVER WOULD HAVE WISHED THE EXPERIENCES SHE'S SINCE GONE THROUGH ON HER.

REGRETTABLY, YES I USE THAT TERM SPECIFICALLY BECAUSE I DO WISH I WAS MORE READILY AVAILABLE TO HER WHENEVER SHE WAS GOING THROUGH ALL OF THIS, I ONLY HAVE SPECIFIC MEMORIES OF TWO INSTANCES THAT I WAS ACTUALLY PRESENT FOR (THOUGH NOT ALWAYS PHYSICALLY), THE FIRST BEING THE INTAKE PROCESS AT THE FACILITY IN INDIANAPOLIS. UNFORTUNATELY, I THINK THAT MY BRAIN IS EITHER GETTING OLD, OR HAS SHUT OUT MOST OF THE ACTUAL SPECIFICS SUBCONSCIOUSLY; THERE ARE NOT AS MANY DETAILS AS I HOPED FOR WHEN I TOLD HER I WOULD TRY TO GIVE HER AN ACCURATE RECOLLECTION OF EVENTS FROM MY OWN POINT OF VIEW.

WHEN I SHOWED UP TO THE FACILITY IN INDIANAPOLIS, THE FIRST THING I RECALL WAS SEEING HER FOR THE FIRST TIME SINCE HER FIRST MANIC EPISODE STARTED. BY THIS TIME, SHE WAS ALREADY A MONTH OR SO INTO IT. BECAUSE I WAS STILL FINISHING MY LAST TWO SEMESTERS AT THE UNIVERSITY OF INDIANAPOLIS (STUPID TRANSFERRING CREDITS), I WASN'T ABLE TO AFFORD—NEITHER FINANCIALLY NOR WITH MY TIME—TO VENTURE DOWN TO EVANSVILLE ANY SOONER. THAT SAID, I WASN'T ENTIRELY SURE WHAT WAS HAPPENING, AS I RECEIVED ALL MY INFORMATION SECONDHAND FROM MOM, WHO I ASSUME WAS TRYING TO KEEP ME FROM WORRYING TOO MUCH. FEELING LIKE IT WAS MISSING THE COMPLETE PICTURE, MY MIND CREATED ITS OWN VISUAL OF HOW JILLIAN MIGHT LOOK WHEN I SAW HER, AND—LUCKILY ENOUGH FOR THE BOTH OF US—WHAT I SAW WAS CONSIDERABLY BETTER THAN THE WORST-CASE SCENARIO MY BRAIN MANAGED

JACOB (Older Brother)

TO INVENT. THE MAIN THING I REMEMBER IS THAT SHE JUST LOOKED TIRED ... JUST ABSOLUTELY MENTALLY, PHYSICALLY, AND EMOTIONALLY EXHAUSTED.

AS FOR ACTUAL INTERACTIONS WITH HER, IT WAS NOTHING LIKE I EXPECTED. NOW, AS STATED BEFORE, ALL MY INFORMATION WAS SECONDHAND, SO I KNEW SHE WAS NOT AS COHERENT AS SHE IS ON A NORMAL BASIS, OR EVEN TO THE LEVEL SHE WAS JUST A FEW DAYS BEFORE. I KNEW SHE WAS SPEAKING MOST OF THAT DAY IN MOVIE QUOTES THAT MOM, AND EVEN MOST OF OUR SIBLINGS (WHO, OF COURSE, CAN TYPICALLY FOLLOW ALONG), DID NOT UNDERSTAND. THAT WAS PROBABLY THE MAIN REASON MOM WANTED ME TO COME ALONG: I WOULD MOST LIKELY UNDERSTAND THE REFERENCES, AND, BETTER STILL, I MIGHT BE ABLE TO RELATE THEM AND INTERPRET HOW THEY MIGHT MAKE SENSE IN THE MOMENT. BASICALLY, I WOULD HAVE A BRIEF, SHINING MOMENT AS JILLIAN'S TRANSLATOR.

HOWEVER, AS I HAD CLASS, I WAS LATE TO MY FIRST DAY ON THE JOB. AS I DROVE TO THE HOSPITAL, I FELT NUMB. BECAUSE I WAS GOING IN BLIND, MY MIND WAS DRAWING A BLANK. WHERE NORMALLY I WOULD HAVE SOME KIND OF EXPECTATION FOR WHERE IT WAS I WAS HEADED, THERE WAS NOTHING ... ASIDE FROM THAT AFOREMENTIONED WORST-CASE VISUAL. TO BE FAIR, EVEN IF MOM SHARED MORE INFORMATION WITH ME, I STILL DON'T THINK I COULD HAVE BEEN PREPARED. WHEN I ENTERED THE FACILITY, AUNT BRITT LED ME TO THE ROOM WHERE SHE, JILLIAN, AND MOM WERE WAITING AFTER THE INITIAL VITALS CHECK.

THE WAITING PERIOD IN THAT ROOM WAS ONE OF THE STRANGEST INTERACTIONS I EVER EXPERIENCED WITH JILLIAN, AND WE HAVEN'T EXACTLY BEEN SHORT ON STRANGE INTERACTIONS, SO THAT IS SAYING A LOT, I BELIEVE. SHE CHOSE TO SIT ON THE OPPOSITE SIDE OF THE TABLE FROM THE THREE OF US, AND SHE HAD THIS BIG BAG. I DIDN'T KNOW WHAT WAS IN IT, BUT I ASSUMED IT WAS JUST SOMETHING SHE AND MOM HAD PUT TOGETHER TO KEEP HER OVERACTIVE BRAIN STIMULATED SO SHE MIGHT NOT BE SO AGITATED. ONE OF THE THINGS IN THE BAG THAT SHE RETRIEVED WAS THIS MASSIVE STACK OF ... I DON'T KNOW WHAT TO CALL THEM. THEY LOOKED LIKE TAROT CARDS, LARGE AND RIGID WITH THESE COLORFUL, ILLUSTRATED DEPICTIONS OF FEMALE CHARACTERS ON THEM. THAT WASN'T THE STRANGE PART TO ME, NOR WAS WHAT SHE WAS DOING WITH THEM, THOUGH THAT WAS DEFINITELY BIZARRE, TOO. SHE WOULD TAKE EACH ONE, (AND THERE HAD TO BE A STACK OF ALMOST 200 CARDS THERE), LOOK AT IT, LOOK AT MOM, LOOK BACK AT THE CARD, LOOK AT ME, LOOK BACK AT THE CARD, LOOK AT AUNT BRITT, LOOK BACK AT THE CARD, AND THEN SOMEHOW ATTRIBUTE SOMETHING WITH THAT CARD TO ONE OF US, AND SAY, "THIS IS YOU," AS SHE'D PLACE IT BEFORE WHOEVER SHE DECIDED THE CARD DESCRIBED. SHE WENT THROUGH THE ENTIRE DECK AND PICKED THEM ALL BACK UP BEFORE THE INTAKE WOMAN EVEN ENTERED THE ROOM.

NOW, LOOKING BACK AT WHAT I REMEMBER AS BEING AN INCREDIBLY STRANGE INTERACTION, IT REALLY DOESN'T SEEM LIKE MUCH TO BE BOTHERED BY, RIGHT? BUT THAT'S THE THING: IT WASN'T EVEN

WHAT SHE WAS DOING THAT WAS DISTURBING (FOR LACK OF A BETTER WORD). IT WAS THE FACT THAT I WAS SITTING THERE WITH MY SISTER PHYSICALLY, BUT THE PERSON THAT WAS THERE WAS NOT MY SISTER. AND WHILE I KNEW SHE WASN'T POSSESSED OR ANYTHING LIKE IT, IT WAS STILL LIKE SOMEONE ELSE HAD TAKEN THE REINS OF HER MIND.

THE INTAKE WOMAN'S NAME ESCAPES ME, I ONLY REMEMBER SHE HAD LONG, DARK HAIR. WHEN SHE FINALLY CAME IN, JILLIAN'S CARD-FLIPPING PERSONA WAS GONE, REPLACED BY SOMEONE WHO SEEMED VERY DISTANT. WHEN SHE'D TURN TO LOOK AT SOMEONE IN THE ROOM, IT WAS MORE LIKE SHE WAS LOOKING THROUGH THEM. A QUIET GLAZE TOOK THE PLACE OF THE FIDGETY, CHATTY PERSON FROM JUST MOMENTS AGO. THROUGHOUT THE INTERVIEW, IT SEEMED LIKE SHE WOULD FLIP BACK AND FORTH BETWEEN THOSE TWO PERSONAS AS THE INTAKE FACILITATOR ASKED QUESTIONS ON QUESTIONS. SOME JILLIAN HAD AN ANSWER FOR, SOME SHE DIDN'T, AND THE THREE OF US WOULD TRY TO ANSWER AS BEST WE COULD.

I REMEMBER THERE WAS ONE MOMENT IN PARTICULAR THAT JILLIAN SAID SOMETHING VERY QUIETLY, AND WHEN SHE WAS ASKED TO REPEAT WHAT SHE SAID, EVERYONE HEARD HER AND IMMEDIATELY TURNED TO ME FOR THE INTERPRETATION, AS IT MADE NO SENSE IN THE CONTEXT. AS I RECALL, IT WAS A DISNEY QUOTE, THOUGH I CAN'T REMEMBER EXACTLY WHICH. AT ANY RATE, I WAS THEN ABLE TO TRANSLATE WHAT SHE WAS TRYING TO SAY FOR THE REST OF THE ROOM.

THE FINAL QUESTION WAS ONE WE COULD NOT ANSWER FOR HER: "DO YOU WANT TO STAY HERE?" AND IN THAT MOMENT, WE ALL SAW SHE KNEW SOMETHING WAS AMISS. THE TWO BATTLING PERSONAS WERE SUDDENLY GONE, AND THERE WAS ALMOST SOME SEMBLANCE OF LUCIDITY. IT WAS THE FIRST TIME I SAW HER EYES FOCUS ON THE PERSON POSING ALL THE QUESTIONS. THE EMOTION IN THEM WAS A CLEAR COMBINATION OF PANIC, EXHAUSTION, AND ... WAS THAT RELIEF? SHE STARTED TEARING UP, AS I AM IN WRITING THIS ... BECAUSE IT WAS SO GUT-WRENCHING TO SEE HER IN THAT WAY, AND JUST SOBBED OUT ONE WORD, "YES."

UNFORTUNATELY, NONE OF US COULD HAVE REALLY KNOWN WHAT TO EXPECT OF THE PLACE AND WHETHER OR NOT THEY WOULD BE HELPFUL HERE. ANYTHING HAD TO HAVE BEEN BETTER THAN THE FIRST HOSPITAL, RIGHT?

AND I AM SORRY WE WERE WRONG.

I WAS FORTUNATE ENOUGH TO BE ABLE TO VISIT JILLIAN ONE MORE TIME (FUCKING PHILOSOPHY NIGHT CLASS KEPT ME FROM BEING ABLE TO VISIT MORE OFTEN) DURING THE COURSE OF HER STAY THERE, BUT SHE WAS IN A MUCH DIFFERENT, SEEMINGLY-BETTER STATE (IN MY OPINION) THAN WHEN SHE FIRST ARRIVED. IT WAS A BRIEF VISIT, BUT I DIDN'T HAVE TO TRANSLATE ANYTHING FOR HER THIS TIME. SHE WAS ABLE TO TELL ME ABOUT SOME OF THE OTHER PATIENTS, ABLE TO CARRY ON A CONVERSATION. SHE LOOKED LIKE SHE WAS FINALLY ABLE TO GET SOME SLEEP, AND HER ENERGY SEEMED SOMEWHAT REPLENISHED.

WHETHER THAT VISIT WAS ONE OF HER MORE "LUCID" VISITS? I CANNOT SAY.

I JUST KNOW THAT I HAVE NEVER BEEN SO RE-LIEVED TO SEE HER CLOSER TO BEING MORE OF THE SISTER THAT I GREW UP WITH.

BROOKE (MOTHER)

The entire four-hour drive to Indianapolis, I spend praying. Oh, and lying. Well, maybe not so much lying as ... shaping the truth.

After a couple of conversations with the helpline, I've gleaned that in order for Jillian to be treated in-patient (Which I see as the only possible option at a hospital four hours from her home), they have to assess that she is a danger to herself or others. This, I'm fairly confident, is a low bar to jump – setting fires, hitchhiking, potentially lethal food preparations – I have a plethora of stories to share that illustrate safety issues. And, of course, she has to agree to the admission since she is an adult.

This is the more challenging bar to clear.

So, I emphasize that the facility bills itself as a "sleep center" and play up the possibility that they can help her with getting the rest she so desperately wants. I truly don't know how perceptive she is in her current state, but I'm certain if she even sniffs that it's anything like the Evansville hospital, she will slam that door shut with emphasis.

As Jake relates quite accurately the details of Jillian's admission interview, I'll leave that as is other than to share my view that her momentary lucid acceptance of admission to the hospital was God's answer to a mother's fervent prayer.

The day after Jillian's admittance to the Indianapolis facility, the assigned social worker calls, and we have an almost hour-long conversation about Jillian's pre-episode personality. Finally, someone who understands that to properly find her baseline, there needs to be some understanding of who Jillian was before her break. Throughout Jillian's hospitalization, the social worker is also in contact with my sister, Britt, on a regular basis and is a ray of sunshine and relatively good information. Maybe we have found the right place to help Jillian!

My first return visit to see Jillian calls my hope into question and is the one that still chills my blood.

As opposed to the Evansville facility, where visitation occurred in the large dining area, the Indianapolis facility allows visitation directly on the unit. After clearing security, I'm directed beyond a locked door to the single floor where Jillian and my sister are waiting in a small room at the far end of the long unit. I am so excited to see her – I miss my daughter terribly – and am so eager to finally see some progress. They sit at a small table working a puzzle. Jillian's dressed in a gown with her hair in braids, and my first impression is that she is floating ... not only in her movements, which are slow and deliberate as she places pieces on the table, but in her focus and behavior. She acknowledges our comments or entreaties ever so slightly in the slow movement of her head in our direction, but she isn't making eye contact or answering and her face is expressionless. She is there, physically, and yet she isn't.

I don't stay long, I can't, because as soon as I reach the outer door of the hospital, the tears come in a torrent.

Later, I learn that her demeanor is a result of the first antipsychotic medicine they were trying, Risperdal, and that it was discontinued when it became apparent that she wasn't responding well. They eventually settle on Seroquel and Invega after trying a couple of other antipsychotics, the names of which escape me.

As before, there aren't any conversations with the doctor directly, not as to diagnosis, medication, treatment plan, nothing. Any morsel of information is funneled through the social worker and – to a lesser degree – the nurses. An improvement, to be sure, but still not completely satisfactory. When Jillian refuses her Invega shot and is taken to court, I'm so thankful my sister attends, but we are both startled (and skeptical) when the doctor testifies that she has settled on a diagnosis of schizophrenia.

SCHIZOPHRENIA.

Since when? Even the social worker is stunned. At no point had this potential diagnosis even been whispered, and we're suspicious that this stigmatizing label has been strategically used as a means to an end. But there it is, and it will destructively echo forward in Jillian's treatment, at least to a point.

There were a few more visits before she was released. When entering the unit, the nurses' station was on your right and they had a view beyond the common area directly in front of their counter continuing down a long "hallway" where the doors to the individual patient rooms were situated, all the way to the end room where I first visited with Jillian. The advantage of this set up was the direct interaction between nurses and patients unlike the Evansville facility where techs acted as gatekeepers. There was a separate "breakroom" kitchenette behind where the nurses worked which is where Jillian and I typically visited. She was back to being chatty, and delusional (some), and combative (to a degree), but frankly this was a relief compared to the zombie state I had witnessed prior.

One day when I arrived for a visit, the nurses were playing the "green glass door" game with Jillian. If you're unfamiliar, it's an elementary school word game for identifying words with double letters. Our entire visit, Jillian's brain was seized with continuing this game. Whenever she or I would speak a double-letter word, she'd immediately remember that word could enter the "door" and become transfixed to add more words to the list.

Another visit, in the midst of a relatively pleasant and promising conversation, she showed me a picture she had painted and confided in all seriousness that she was certain we could sell it for a large sum of money. Now, my daughter is artistic … but this wasn't a masterpiece by any stretch of the imagination.

((Until the publication of this book, that is. I've still got it, who wants it?))

As our visits continued, she slowly moved closer to baseline, but it seemed as if she could only get so far. The social worker advised that we were near a point where for Jillian to progress, she needed to be moved out of this particular unit in the hope of soon releasing her. After trying to step her up to a different unit with more interaction and group sessions, her anxiety kicked in and · threatened to reverse her progress. They relented and sent her back to her original unit. It wasn't too long after that she was released and another leg of this seemingly-endless journey begins.

BRITT
(AUNT/BROOKE'S SISTER)

Jillian has always been an extremely intelligent, imaginative, and witty person. She continuously found ways to express herself creatively – through dancing, singing, acting, and writing, starting from childhood and beyond – so it came as no surprise to me when she chose to study the arts in college.

I have collected many funny stories about my oldest niece throughout the years. One of my favorites is when she was maybe 7 or 8, she told her mom a joke, and apparently, her mom either didn't think it was funny or wasn't amused enough to satisfy Jillian's expectations, so Jillian asked Brooke if she could call me and tell me her joke instead because, "Aunt Britt laughs at everything!" (Which is true. I'm easily amused.)

Jillian's mom, my older sister, and I are very close. As I have been on this journey with Brooke, my understanding of how incredibly strong my sister is has only solidified further. It was downright scary when Jillian went into the first hospital in Evansville. The doctors and nurses were not allowed to speak with Brooke about what was happening, medically, with her daughter. But they didn't know Jillian the way her mom knows her, didn't know her personality. They didn't know about her wittiness and occasional, biting sarcasm. They didn't know her humor. As they were drugging her in different ways, how were they supposed to know when they landed at *Jillian*???

While Jillian was at the second hospital, the one in Indianapolis, I made every effort to visit her as often as I was allowed. She and I would talk about a lot of different things.

There was one instance in particular, when I was visiting, that she and I were sitting in the living area with several of the other patients, who were laughing and recounting things that had happened throughout the day. I was listening along and chuckling at various quips when, at one point, Jillian said something so off-the-wall impossible (I only wish I could give you a direct quote) that I thought, *Well, wait a second. There's no way that happened. Hold on a moment ...*

I turned to the nearest nurse,

"Did *any* of these things happen today?"

She gave a knowing smile.

"No."

This was a very bizarre experience. The patients were so believable! I began to think more deeply about the concept of reality. What is reality? How do we know what is real or make-believe?

Often during our visits, Jillian would become obsessed with telling me how she was counting down the days until she left, which concerned me because

I didn't think she was ready to be without care. She was not herself. She was still quoting song lyrics and/ or movies, still paranoid. Dr. S___ had been trying to stabilize her with different medications, and they never seemed to be landing on the right combination. She either wasn't sleeping or she was sleeping too much, practically catatonic at one point. She would tell me over and over again how she was not going to take any medication when she left the hospital because she hated the doctor. I knew how bad it had gotten for her before she went into the hospital, and I was concerned for her health and safety if she left too soon.

Apparently, the doctor had similar concerns because the hospital filed for Jillian to be committed for additional days.

I went to the courthouse on the day of the hearing, the only family member able to attend. Jillian was waiting for me, and I remember she was wearing her own clothes as opposed to the clothes given her by the facility; she had on her cute little tennis shoes that she had worn into the hospital the night she signed herself in. I didn't know whether Jillian had ever been in a courtroom, which can be intimidating, but she seemed calm. It quickly became clear to me that she definitely had no idea why she was in a courtroom; she seemed lost. She did not understand what we were doing there or that it was a hearing to try to have her committed to the hospital, which – if successful – would keep her in for an extended amount of time. She would lose her voluntary status and no longer be allowed to sign herself out.

The most vivid memory I have about the hearing was when Dr. S___ was on the stand testifying. I remember her telling the Judge that Jillian was a bright young lady with many years ahead of her, and she was concerned that if Jillian left the hospital, she would go untreated, and **the longer a person goes untreated, the less likely that person is to return to their baseline personality.**

The Judge ultimately signed the commitment papers, and Jillian returned to treatment.

A huge takeaway from the entire experience (especially that of the first hospital): After witnessing firsthand how helpless parents are in this type of situation, my husband and I asked all of our adult children to sign a Power of Attorney document that would give us the ability to confer with medical personnel and/or make decisions on our children's behalf, should they become incapacitated in their adult lives. After watching how frightening it was for my sister and her oldest daughter, how powerless Brooke felt when trying to obtain just a modicum of information as to Jillian's welfare, I wanted to be absolutely certain nothing quite so terrifying would happen to any of my own children.

Perhaps we didn't learn these life lessons the way any of us planned to (they're certainly lessons I wouldn't wish on *anyone*), but I must say, I'm glad we were able to learn them before anything happened to someone who may not have as much stubborn resilience as my oldest niece. I am thankful for her continuing recovery. I am also thankful for modern medicine, but we have a long way to go with addressing mental healthcare and understanding the brain. Though Jillian's experiences were more difficult than I think she sometimes lets on (or has the capacity to tell us), I'm so happy to see her turn them into something that may help other people going through similar events.

JENNA
(YOUNGER SISTER/PSYCH NURSE)

Due to being swamped in Evansville with my aforementioned array of activities (nursing, work, cheer, gymnastics, life, etc.), I was not as involved in Jillian's Indianapolis stay. I received updates from Mom, and it seemed as though some of the euphoria was resolving ... but Jillian was crashing back down.

Hard.

She was becoming beyond depressed, exhausted, downright miserable. On the flipside, I—to be completely honest—was somewhat relieved. Not that I would ever want her to suffer (obviously), but it was a change I had been hoping for because I was starting to worry that she was truly stuck. Given that I was in the beginning stages of nursing school, I knew enough to research the *likelihood* of what to expect, but there's no amount of research about mental illness that lets you KNOW what to expect beyond any shadow of a doubt.

Of course, Jillian's doctors also kept switching the diagnoses around and the causes seemed to be up in the air as well. So, I was researching *everything:* K2, serotonin syndrome, bipolar disorder, schizophrenia, marijuana ... I was reading all the information I possibly could and trying to connect the dots for myself.

I honestly was convinced she had gotten ahold of synthetic weed (K2) for a hot minute and had truly ruined her brain, as none of the antipsychotics they kept trying seemed to work. And I had read a truly terrifying article about a young man that never came out of his psychosis after smoking K2, so when there was a shift from euphoria to *anything* else, I was hoping it was a sign I was wrong.

CHAPTER SIX

In September, I finally returned home on medications that mostly imprisoned me in a depressed daze. Exorbitant amounts of Seroquel kept me heavy and numb.

I didn't receive a proper diagnosis until October. I remember a very fuzzy (and probably incorrect) general sequence of events.

My mother took me to see Dr. A _ _ _ at Evansville Psychiatric Associates for a few appointments, none of which I have any memory. She told me that he immediately recognized I was on far too high a dose of Seroquel, though I can't recall if he lowered it immediately or not.

The Indianapolis hospital had forwarded my hospital records (I still haven't seen those. I'm sure they're a trip.), but the Evansville hospital did not. This proved to be problematic, as Evansville Psychiatric Associates only had access to the notes from a doctor who misdiagnosed me and were unable to view the notes from the start of the episode. They were not operating with a complete picture.

Granted, I'm not certain the notes would've helped too much, given the fact that I left *that* hospital with an entirely ambiguous diagnosis, but more information certainly wouldn't have hurt as much as the lesser amount of information did.

In the beginning of October, Dr. A _ _ _ referred me to a Dr. B _ _ _ for a more-involved Psychologist Intake Questionnaire. He was to administer a 500-question, fill-in-the-bubble quiz in order to determine whether or not my current diagnosis was accurate.

I don't believe I had to answer all 500 questions, but it certainly didn't make it seem any less agonizing.

The questions were all over the place:

> *Do you have an interest in architecture?*

> *Do you enjoy being in nature?*

> *Do you think your neighbors are following you?*

I answered the questions I was assigned to the best of my ability, and a few days later (I think) I returned to see Dr. B _ _ _ for my results. Who doesn't love a good judgment day?

"Well, I don't know how truthful you were in answering your survey. The results for your test came back inconclusive, so unfortunately I'm going to have to stick with your original diagnosis of schizophrenia."

This is when I lost it.

I'd been pretty numb beyond repair up to this point in time, but that result would be the prodigious straw that broke the camel's back.

I burst into tears. The uncontrollable kind.

"I'm not. I'm not crazy. I don't know how to tell you, I don't know how to convince *anyone*, but I've been trying to for weeks. I'm not schizophrenic, I'm not crazy."

When I get back into acting eventually (again), I know I'll be able to summon tears every time I go back to that feeling, to that exact moment.

That was despair. Utter hopelessness. Defeat.

I'd been through sheer hell and fought with everything I had to keep my sanity, to keep my life itself, and I was met with "Game Over."

And I had nothing left to fight with.

Perhaps that would've been the end of me altogether, if not for the nagging feeling that Dr. B _ _ _ supposably had after that meeting.

My mom and I left, and she persuaded me into going for a walk. It was on said walk that Dr. B _ _ _ called her phone.

> "I don't normally do this, but I would like you to come in and take the test again."

You have got to be kidding me.

I went back to the office to retake that endless survey, but before I started this time, Dr. B _ _ _ said,

> "Perhaps I should have asked you this last time. But do you see any people that aren't really present?"

> "No."

> "Do you hear any voices that no one else hears?"

> "No."

> "Okay. Go ahead and start your quiz."

I haven't the faintest idea of how the results were any different from the first go-round, but Dr. B _ _ _ decided they were not the same because suddenly,

> "You have bipolar disorder. Most likely Bipolar I."

Fine. Great. Whatever. If you have to stick some kind of label on me, we'll go with that. I'll be bipolar if that's what it takes to cut this crap out.

October and November are more empty holes in my memory, which takes us to December.

Imagine, if you will, how a Christmas performing contract might go.

If you imagined, "Not well at all," then you are astute.

My performance job was mainly to greet guests for their walkthrough of a giant, inflatable version of "A Christmas Carol". I was standing for hours on end, in the dead of winter, in the doorway of a "heated" outdoor pavilion (I apparently had a different understanding of the word "heated."), in period costume, and smiling, waving, and serving the most hollowed out "Welcome" of all time.

You don't know Dead Inside until you've been through the ringer of hospitalizations and then go on to work a job where you have to wish people a "Merry Christmas," pretending things are COMPLETELY FINE while drugging yourself into a stupor every night with medications that are not actually helping you.

Talk about POST Post Traumatic Stress.

The contract was in a beautiful hotel in Kentucky, and perhaps—had I not been so heavily-medicated and depressed—I would've been able to make some lifelong friends.

The reality, however, was that I would drive to McDonald's each day after my shift ended and try to eat my feelings, followed by a shower in which I would sit on the floor of the tub and sob for hours, followed immediately by a cocktail of prescription drugs and far too much sleep. I was in bed between 6 and 7 PM every night.

Even TV was a no-go because you know what would be on TV after the end of my shift? *Seinfeld.* Freaking *Seinfeld.* I could never—and I'm going to guess **will** never—understand the appeal. And I really tried during this Christmas contract, believe you me. I gave it my best shot, absolutely desperate for a distraction. No luck.

I couldn't talk to anyone—who could possibly understand what I was going through? None of the performers I was working with, I'm certain.

They were having cheerful Christmas parties and screening musicals with sing-alongs.

I was trying not to kill myself.

We were not in the same place.

I called home and sobbed to my mother *every single day.* I would drive home almost every weekend, a four-hour drive round trip. I was miserable. I was gaining weight. I was oversleeping. I was isolated.

I was dying.

And my job was to wish people a "Merry Christmas".

Should I have worked the contract? Absolutely not. But I had signed on well before any hospitalization was even on the horizon, and I was afraid that if I backed out, it was going to tank my performing career. I would be forever known as a flake.

Instead, I was known as a nightmare. *Nice save, Jillian.*

Christmas 2014 could not pass by quickly enough.

Eventually it did, and only a few things were able to pull me back from the edge of the abyss where I found myself standing:

1. Most importantly, a correct treatment plan. Because it was going to take so long to taper the dose of Seroquel and subsequently tweak adjustments for a mood-stabilizer, Dr. A _ _ _ reluctantly left me on Seroquel throughout the Christmas contract. It made him too nervous to do too much fine-tuning when

I was set to be on my own out
of state in only a few weeks.[**]

2.   A job working with children.
      How on earth did you land a job
      working with kids? Sheer luck.
      Thankfully, the Montessori I
      worked at for 2 years was none
      the wiser[***], and it truly healed
      me to be working that job every
      day. Kids are miracle workers.

3.   Performing. Eventually, being
      on the correct treatment plan
      and working with kids led me
      to a more stable place emotion-
      ally and mentally, and I had the
      ability to get back in the sad-
      dle with performing.

2015 was a healing year for me. Spiri-
tually, physically, mentally, emotionally,
you name it.

Throughout the aforementioned Christmas contract, because Dr. A _ _ _ did not
like the idea of trying to adjust my meds
while I was alone and out of state, I was
on three or four different medications. To

[**] So, this is technically true? But there are some
inaccuracies to be corrected.
[***] Staff was routinely asked what medications we
were on, and I would routinely lie. I wanted to
keep my job, thank you very much.

start, I was on an insane dose of Seroquel. Seroquel is an SGA (second generation antipsychotic or atypical antipsychotic) intended to treat schizophrenia. It is often used to sedate patients. Unfortunately, the Seroquel was making me suicidal, so I was also prescribed Wellbutrin (an antidepressant). Alas, Wellbutrin drastically affected my blood pressure and caused the worst restless leg syndrome I ever experienced. I was prescribed a third medication to help with that, namely Propranolol (a Beta blocker). It was a never-ending avalanche of medication after medication after medication. C was to fight the side effects of B, and B was only prescribed to fight the side effects of A, and A was treating the wrong diagnosis from the get-go.

How on Earth this delightful little blend of pills on pills on pills resulted in a deep depression is really beyond me.

Once my contract ended, however, Dr. A _ _ _ sprang into action. He immediately stopped the horse doses of Seroquel and decided to give Lithium (the most commonly prescribed mood stabilizer) a go.

I did not and still do not like Lithium.

But it does get me back to a more stable equilibrium. It gives the doctors the ability to determine where my baseline is supposed to be. I can't knock it for that.

But the side effects? I can knock it for the side effects.

Before my first episode, the heaviest I'd ever been was 125 lbs.

After my first episode and my first go-round with Lithium, I ballooned to 188.

Call it vanity, but I did not want to weigh close to 200 pounds, when I'd been so slim my entire life.

It was, after all, the outcome of my hospitalization I was unable to hide. I could bury the mental, emotional, psychological trauma (not in a healthy way, obviously), but I could not hide this.

It certainly didn't do anything to help with the onslaught of depression as I was still reeling in the aftermath of the first manic episode. Neither did the other side effects, for that matter: brain fog, memory loss, total apathy, trouble concentrating. The list goes on and on.

I'd lost friends. I'd gained nearly 70 pounds. Any money I made on that Charlottesville theatrical contract was long gone. I'd spent it while manic. I had no source of income now that the Christmas contract was up, and I was practically unemployable.

But I was officially not schizophrenic.

What a silver lining.

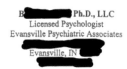

B[redacted] Ph.D., LLC
Licensed Psychologist
Evansville Psychiatric Associates
Evansville, IN [redacted]

A[redacted] M.D.
Evansville, IN [redacted]

RE: **Jillian Weinzapfel** [redacted]

Dear Dr. A[redacted]

Thank you for the referral of 22-year-old Jillian Weinzapfel for Psychological Testing. She was seen by me on 10-02-2014 for administration of select psychological tests, after review of personal background documented in the company file as well as that reported by her on the present Psychologist Intake Questionnaire. Your reason for referral for testing using norm-referenced psychological measures was to gather empirical data to clarify psychiatric diagnoses, particularly a psychotic disorder. When asked about her current concerns, Jillian stated, "I don't much have difficulties anymore, but what happened was that I had a 'psychotic break' one night while smoking marijuana and taking Celexa." She denies any present problems of thinking like hallucinations, delusions, or any other unrealistic ideas or sensations. She does not agree with the diagnosis of 'undifferentiated schizophrenia' assigned by [redacted] in Indianapolis (which discharged her to current outpatient care locally). Jillian believes that a more likely possibility diagnostically is an underlying depression that she's experienced before, or some kind of mood disorder ("even Bipolar"). She states, "My academic advisor in college, who I shared a lot with, felt that my moods went to extremes".

These psychological tests were completed in the present assessment: Beck Depression Inventory-Second edition (BDI-II);   Adult Manifest Anxiety Scale-All adults (AMAS-A); Minnesota Multiphasic Personality Inventory-2 (MMPI-2);   MoodCheck screening form (MC).

(NOTE: JILLIAN HAS MAINTAINED USE OF HER PRESCRIBED MEDICATIONS, SO THEIR INFLUENCE IS PRESUMED TO BE PRESENT IN THIS TESTING.)

On the **BDI-II**, a self-rating measure pertaining to depressive or discouraged symptoms experienced by her at present, the derived total score of 11 registered within the 'Minimal' range (scores from 0 to 13) in reference to depressiveness, according to norms for adults. In other words, she identified a set of variously-weighted symptoms that added together would reflect neither a significant/clinical depression, nor a burden beyond what might be experienced as typical for 'average' adults. For the record, in association with the symptom domain of suicidal thoughts/wishes, she endorsed the following specific item: 'I don't have any thoughts of killing myself'. But she did endorse these items with values/intensities greater than nil, and conveying 'qualitatively' a message of some depressiveness that can't be ignored: I feel sad (some) of the time; I don't enjoy things as much as I used to; I have lost confidence in myself; I feel more restless or wound up than usual; I am less interested in other people or things than before; I find it more difficult to make decisions than usual; I don't consider myself as worthwhile and useful as I used to; I sleep somewhat more than usual; I am more irritable than usual; My appetite is somewhat greater than usual; I can't concentrate as well as usual.

On the **AMAS-A**, a measure of self-perceptions regarding anxious/worried/fearful feelings and behaviors currently acknowledged by her, scores varied for the three component Subscales--ranging from 'normal' to mildly or moderately elevated when gauged by norms for other adults. These specific results were obtained: Worry/Oversensitivity Subscale 55T (a mild elevation);   Physiological Anxiety Subscale 65T (a moderate elevation);   Social Concerns/ Stress Subscale 51T (an average outcome).   Her style of responding was found to be acceptably consistent per the instrument's validity index (scoring at 54T), lending credence to her responses in general.

The self-descriptive **MMPI-2** is a personality measure exploring many dimensions of one's psychology through both obvious and indirect questions. Analysis first of her validity scale outcomes yielded no indication of significant bias in being overly-positive, overly-negative, or inconsistent in her manner or attitude of responding. Accordingly, attention was then directed to any clinical scale results which exceeded the standard criterion for interpretation (i.e., scores above 70T, or over two standard deviations above the instrument's Mean of 50T). Three clinical scales' scores qualified for focused interpretation--Scale 2 (associated with depression) at 77T; Scale 7 (affiliated with anxiety) at 75T; and Scale 4 (related to rebelliousness) at a marginal 71T. Her peak score of 77T on Scale 2 is typically reflective of a person displaying depressive symptoms, that might include sadness, vulnerability to having one's feelings easily hurt, irritability, and easy fatigue and loss of energy. A high score often leads to a diagnosis of depression. And then, her T-score of 75 on Scale 7 suggests psychological tension and discomfort, typically manifesting in nervousness/anxiety, fearfulness and apprehension, and possible agitation. A person producing such an elevated score may feel guilty about not living up to one's own standards, and depressed about falling short of goals. Finally, the slightly-elevated 71T scored on Scale 4 may reflect some rebelliousness of feelings or behaviors, likely in passive or indirect ways. A history of stormy relationships with family members may be present. This individual may also be impatient, have limited frustration tolerance, and behave at times with poor judgment. Yet it must be noted that scores on Scale 4 tend to be related to age, with younger persons scoring slightly higher than older persons.

The **MC** form was administered to Jillian after the initial round of testing, and it was not billed. It is not a norm-referenced measure, but still its findings can be illuminating, especially when wondering about mood cycling or swings. She did endorse with a checkmark the following statements as accurately describing herself (and per instructions, applying to times when she was not using drugs or alcohol):   I notice that my mood and/or energy levels shift drastically from time to time;   At times, I am moody and/or energy level is very low, and at other times, very high; During my 'low' phases, I often feel a lack of energy, a need to stay in bed or get extra sleep, and little or no motivation to do things I need to do; During my low phases, I often feel 'blue', sad all the time, or depressed; Sometimes during the low phases, I feel helpless or even suicidal; During the low phases, my ability to function at work or socially is impaired; Typically, the low phases last for a few weeks, but sometimes they last only a few days; I also experience a period of 'normal' mood in between mood swings, during which my mood and energy level feels 'right' and my ability to function is not disturbed; During 'high' periods, I feel irritable, 'on edge', or aggressive; During the high periods, I may take on too many activities at once; During the high periods, I may spend money in ways that cause me trouble; I may be more talkative, outgoing, or sexual during these periods; Sometimes, my behavior during the high periods seems strange or annoying to others. Then, when later elaborating on her depressive experiences on this form, Jillian acknowledged the following: being in Grade School when she was first depressed; having greater than 10 episodes of depression; finding antidepressant medicine (she's only tried one) to have caused excessive energy and racing thoughts; and in episodes of depression, finding that she has lost contact with reality (e.g., delusions, voices, people thought she was odd).

Conclusions and Recommendations:

Neither Jillian's current presentation nor test outcomes (especially on the MMPI-2 pertaining to personality structure and processes) are suggestive of schizophrenia.

Consideration was then given to her experiencing over the last few months and probably longer, a Depressive Disorder Not Otherwise Specified. This could incorporate depressive features but also anxious ones, and when experienced in extremes (like during a major depressive episode showing psychotic aspects), might disrupt thinking and judgment. But her endorsed descriptions of self on the MC form lead me to strongly suspect a Mood Disorder Not Otherwise Specified (DSM-IV code: 296.90), which also could incorporate the features cited above, as well as mood swings.

I would encourage Jillian to continue in your psychiatric care. I believe the results of this Testing offer much for further consideration as you manage and adjust her medicine.

I appreciate having had the opportunity to assess Jillian Weinzapfel in this Psychological Testing. The findings from this assessment will be shared with her by me.

Sincerely,

B▪▪▪▪▪▪ Ph.D., HSPP
Indiana Licensed Psychologist
Health Service Provider in Psychology

BROOKE (MOTHER)

When Jillian returned to Evansville, she was decidedly less chatty, but she also wasn't delusional or psychotic, so there was that for the "pros" column. Unfortunately, she still wasn't well by any means. And I still wasn't buying the "schizophrenic" diagnosis, so it was time to continue searching for real answers.

In the meantime, Jillian met with the same Evansville LCSW, Amy, she was seeing before she left for Indianapolis (you know, her "mom"). After seeing Jillian in her drugged-up state, she referred us to a psychiatrist for assistance in modifying Jillian's medications. Dr. A___ immediately agreed with Amy's assessment and promptly nixed the Invega shots and soon after began lowering the Seroquel doses.

He then ordered the psychological assessment with Dr. B___, the saga which Jillian accurately relates, to which I would only add my strong belief that any patient suffering from a mental health illness, particularly when in the throes of a crisis, needs to have an advocate walking with them every step of the way through the healthcare world. Prior to this experience, I considered a person's mental health treatment as something to only be shared between doctor and patient. But if you think of it in terms of a serious illness, say like cancer, and the person suffering the illness can't participate fully – maybe because of the illness itself or even due to the exhausting mental toll of coming to terms with the fact of the illness – then it becomes clear that the patient needs not just the love and support of family, but an advocate with the strength and perspective to question and push back when well-meaning healthcare professionals miss the mark.

To wit, while Jillian was in Indianapolis, and frustrated by a lack of information from any of her healthcare professionals as to what was happening to her, I began searching for information online and turned to my old friends: books.

I came across one written by a Canadian mother who detailed her journey looking for help with her mentally ill daughter. It was titled "After Her Brain Broke" by Susan Inman, and it opened my eyes and pointed me toward the National Alliance for the Mentally Ill (NAMI) organization. Lo and behold, there was a chapter in our community and a nine-week nighttime educational course was beginning just a few days after Jillian's return home. After arranging with my mother to stay each week with Jillian and her younger siblings, I immersed myself in the information and learned volumes – not only from the two lovely ladies who facilitated the evidence-based course, but also – from the other participants, many like me, family to a person experiencing mental illness, and some who themselves suffered from mental illness and were trying to make sense of their experiences or help others be advocates for fellow sufferers. There is power in knowledge, right? And I was beginning to find my feet after so many weeks of shifting sands.

It was during this course that I experienced what the facilitators predicted would happen more than once during the lessons – my "Aha!" moments.

The first came about three weeks in when we learned the basic symptomology of several major mental illnesses, based on the diagnostic manual used by the medical profession. Starting with schizophrenia, and then onto major depressive disorder and bipolar disorder, as well as some maybe-less-prevalent disorders, we moved through a checklist of symptoms and likely behaviors associated with each brain disease. Schizophrenia didn't clearly line up, neither did major depressive disorder, but when we came to the list of symptoms for bipolar, I could easily check 90 percent of the behaviors. Even though I was not familiar at that time with the term "word salad", I knew exactly what was being described. Finally, a description for those disconnected "conversations"! And I first learned that a person suffering from bipolar disorder could experience psychosis and even hallucinations, both of which I'd always associated only with schizophrenia, based on my limited understanding of that disease. A seed was planted.

My next "Aha!" was a couple evenings later when we reviewed a list of psychiatric medications by category, each listed with what was termed the *primary negative side effects*. Another eye-opener, the anti-depressant that Jillian had been prescribed and doubled up the night of her first episode was one of a few that could be "activating" – meaning it could result in mania if the person taking it was predisposed to such a reaction. Wait, what? Added to what we had already seen in our NAMI materials regarding the close correlation between marijuana and psychosis, now that seed has sprouted.

Back to the books. This NAMI group had a collection, and I began reading about the life experiences of women who had battled bipolar disorder starting with "An Unquiet Mind" and "Touched with Fire" by Dr. Kay Redfield Jamison, a clinical psychologist and researcher who suffers the disorder, although not until after she had been working in the field for quite some time. Her ability to describe her experiences from a clinical and personal viewpoint is riveting and illuminating. Then I flew through "A Brilliant Madness" and "Call Me Anna" by Patty Duke. But the other biography that made a strong impression was "Skywriting, A Life Out of the Blue" by Jane Pauley in which she details her midlife discovery that she is bipolar after a cortisone shot elicits a hypomanic episode and she is later stabilized with Lithium and other meds. She had lived 50-plus years of a successful, very public life seemingly without a whiff of this underlying condition, and with one inadvertent chemical, she falls into bipolar quicksand. I'm ready to move my plant out in the sun and see if it thrives.

Sometime after this, Jillian sees Dr. A___ and undergoes the psychological testing with Dr. B___. Although I hadn't yet shared my budding thoughts with any of her healthcare providers, I'm listening and watching, and the day she receives her testing "results" is the first time I push back.

They are the experts when it comes to medicines and the brain diseases, I know this, but I'm an expert on my daughter, and they don't have benefit of knowing her baseline and progression. Dr. B___'s initial reluctance to part with the Indy doctor as to diagnosis is, in my opinion, spineless, however well-meaning, but I'm pleased when after relating some facts that he apparently wasn't privy

135

to prior to testing and pleading her case, he's moved that day to look further. I will be forever grateful for his professional integrity.

Jillian's next appointment with Dr. A___ is a few days away. She's driving now and slowly recovering although not able to read or really occupy herself in any meaningful way ... probably why this time period is much a blur to her. This is something that has struck me after her episodes: A good measure of how far along she is in recovering is whether she can or will read. Not sure if this is a sign of more organized thought, the dissipation of Invega or other drugs from her system, or a symptom of her post-episode depression. Maybe all of it. But as the younger siblings are back in school and I attempt to get back to my professional obligations, she hangs out at home. Until one afternoon, she calls me at the office to tell me in a detached and calm manner that she is having suicidal thoughts. Unfortunately, some of the medicines used in psychiatric care list this as a possible side effect and I had been in the habit of googling her medicines to keep up on the possibilities. One of the medicines she has recently been prescribed (I wish I could remember which one) included this side effect.

The fact that she recognizes these thoughts for what they are, ideation, is a little reassuring, so I ask if she feels up to driving to the office and that we will call her doctor's office to see if she should stop taking this recently-added medication. She arrives shortly, and the nurse on call advises to stop the recently-added medicine and adds that Dr. A___ wants her to report to yet another local facility. By this time, I've learned the system. It's late afternoon, so once we arrive nursing staff will likely evaluate her, put her to bed, and she won't be seen until the morning by Dr. A___, if then. And it'll be a massive fight to get her to agree to yet another hospital.

Or.

She can sleep at home in my bed with me, and she has an appointment early the next morning with Amy who can help us evaluate our options and we can go from there. Dr. A___'s nurse isn't pleased, but I make the call to keep her home at least tonight.

At the appointment, Amy agrees that Jillian doesn't appear to be a threat to herself but that, in the meantime, she probably needs to have some sort of care during the days I'm at work. The same facility that Dr. A___ had suggested the afternoon before has a day care option, so we head there to discuss this possibility. After an evaluation, they invite Jillian to admit herself, which she most emphatically declines, but she does reluctantly agree to go there during the daytime hours.

After a couple of days, a nurse practitioner shares with me her professional opinion that Jillian is bipolar and should be migrated to Lithium. As this aligned with Dr. B___ and what I had learned through NAMI, I ask what that would entail. She informs me that it will require Jillian to be admitted, probably for a week or two. *There's no way she will agree*, is all I could think. Jillian has been looking forward to her upcoming theatrical stint in Louisville, a beacon of normalcy, and this would be in direct conflict ... besides the complete impossibility that she would give her consent.

In the meantime, Dr. A___ has sent an official letter informing that he would be discontinuing his services due to Jillian's failure not to follow his hospitalization recommendation, although he would keep the appointment the next week, and that she should find a new psychiatrist.

As if it hasn't been difficult enough to walk this journey, now this. Add it to the list of what's wrong with mental healthcare – that a patient must follow the doctor's recommendation as to a course of treatment or be fired. Can you imagine this with any other chronic disease?

At the "final" appointment, we go over my decision to keep her at home and Dr. A___ relents when I insist that it isn't his patient, Jillian, who didn't cooperate but that I made the choice for her. He shares a story of a prior patient who had committed suicide and his faulty evaluation that the patient wouldn't carry it out. Whether he had already reconsidered his "firing" Jillian or my confession gave him the out he was looking for to save face, I couldn't say, maybe he simply sensed my desperation, but he retained Jillian.

We share the nurse practitioner's assessment and recommendation as to Lithium, and to my surprise Dr. A___ concurs. When I also relay her opinion that this change would require hospitalization, Dr. A___ surprises again. He says, "We can start it today." Really?! This is another confusing aspect of mental healthcare – the sometimes-wide divergence between caregivers as to what is possible or what they are each comfortable in offering. He calls it in, and it is done. For the time being, and in light of her Louisville commitment, he keeps her on Seroquel and another anxiety medicine, as it will take some time for the Lithium to reach a therapeutic level. Maybe it is finally time to harvest the plant from that tiny NAMI seed. There's a very faint light at the end of an oh-so-long tunnel.

CHAPTER SEVEN

I'm not sure if starting another chapter here is the answer, but I'm going for it. Feels right.

Listen, we've accepted I don't know how to write a book. If you've made it this far, kudos. Maybe it's more entertaining than I thought. Entertaining may be the wrong word. Gripping? Insightful? Genius? Better than cleaning the house?

I'll take what I can get.

I worked irregularly, for a time, doing data entry jobs in my mom's accounting office. Nothing big, but something to at least try and get back into the swing of "regular" (non-hospitalized) life.

Up to that point, I hadn't worked many jobs outside of performing. I worked as a filing clerk in my dad's pediatric office, and I filed at my mom's office. I worked VERY briefly in a factory—per my parents' suggestion (It was supposed to educate me about how important it was to get my college education. Don't ask. As weird as what you're imagining, and then still probably worse.). I babysat here and there. I sang at Church once in a while for $20 a mass.

That was my entire résumé.

Not super impressive.

Before I picked up my life-saving job at Montessori Academy, I had a couple of brief stints at a Donut Bank Bakery (Hated it. I lasted maybe three weeks tops. To be completely candid, I was still eating my feelings. Unlimited access to donuts I wasn't supposed to be ingesting was not helping my weight struggles. Imagine that.) and then also at a Pet Food Center. I can't believe I almost forgot about that.

I flooded the fish area.

In my defense, I told the managing associate who moved me to the "animal section" that I was not trained to be back there, that I had only ever worked the register, and he chose to ignore me.

It was my very last shift, as my two weeks' notice was already filed, and I decided—unintentionally, I assure you—to go out with a bang.

Or a flood, rather.

Thankfully, I was already employed at Montessori.

Furthermore, thankfully Montessori was desperate and had a high turnover rate.

I considered Montessori to be my first "real" job. It was the longest I'd been employed in my life to that point, and it was a job that I acquired striking out on my own and following up on a newspaper "Help Wanted" ad. It wasn't a performing job. It wasn't working for someone in the family. It was a steady, full-time job.

And it was preposterous.

The starting wage for a classroom assistant was $8.50/hr. After 2 years of employment, I didn't even see a full $1 raise. I think I was given a 10¢ raise every 6 months if memory serves? Golly gee, I wonder why turnover was so high? Who doesn't want to work a thankless job with tons of children, where you're not allowed to sit down or say "No" and have to always present a quiet, neutral tone of voice/facial expression, doing far more physically demanding work than most of the teachers (who are being paid far more than you and are allowed to sit down and not work after hours/holidays) all while making the BAREST minimum wage with no benefits and teeny-tiny raises?

Not everything was all bad, obviously, or I wouldn't have stuck around for 2 years. I hate to sound as though I'm ungrateful for my time there. The pay scale at the time may have been inadequate, but I really loved the people. The director and assistant director, the teacher I worked with (and some that I didn't), the other classroom assistants in the trenches with me—some of the kindest women I've ever met.

I'd work there again in a heartbeat … so long as the pay improved. Hugely.

The pay and the workload may not have been sunshine and roses, but working with those kids turned my life right around.

I was a C E L E B R I T Y at that school.

"Ms. Jillian, Ms. Jillian!" rang out every time I entered a room.

Those kids loved me.

And boy was I in dire need of some unconditional love.

I started that job in a very dark, very different place than where I ended it.

By the end of my time at Montessori, I was back to weighing in around 125, and I had quit Lithium.

RECORD SCRATCH

Yes, I had stopped taking Lithium. Was I supposed to? No, I was not.

There were a few things happening simultaneously as I was recovering from my first manic episode and hospitalization. I started working at Montessori, and that was doing wonders in and of itself.

But about a month into the job, I decided to also audition for a musical at Evansville Civic Theatre. I don't know if you're familiar with the classic *Oklahoma!,* but I took a leap of faith and turned up at auditions.

I somehow managed to land the lead, far beyond anything I anticipated.

I was aiming for a role in the chorus, scout's honor. I knew all the singing and dancing in that show was going to be good for me, and I was more than happy to be in the background.

When I read that I was cast as Laurey Williams, I cried.

At the time of the audition, I was still taking Lithium, and it very much numbed me emotionally and stunted me creatively. I become apathetic when taking it, and—assuming that I would be taking it for the rest of my life—I imagined acting was going to become near-impossible. How was I supposed to create any believable emotions to reflect the inner turmoil of my characters when I was so flat and listless? Everything would feel contrived, and I would feel like a sham. Perhaps no one in the audience would be able to see through the double layer of insincerity, but I would know it was entirely faked.

It's an interesting thing about acting, and I know this may make me seem pompous, but bear with me here: People unfamiliar with the psychology of acting believe that actors are very good *liars*. Very good at *faking* emotions. To some extent, I'm certain that is true. There are many actors who—for all intents and purposes—have seen success going that route. But we've all seen what happens when an actor *truthfully* connects to the emotions, to the psychological intentions and motivations behind *WHY* a character is saying or doing something—it takes the art to a new level totally.

So, to really seal the deal on how pretentious I am regarding my own performance: If I don't connect to the material and deliver an honest, truthful, vulnerable performance, I am a fraud.

Lithium would make me a phony forever.

My entire life plan was officially in the garbage bin. Until that very audition. Something as simple as a lead role in a community theatre production of *Oklahoma!* was more than enough for me to decide *Perhaps I don't have to throw in the towel just yet.*

I won't bore you with the details of the show necessarily, but I will say, I'm truly grateful that I was cast. Not only did I recant my resignation from my dreams, but I also met my future husband.

That's right.

This maniac is married. And her husband is (mostly) sane.

JEFFREY (HUSBAND)

From the very beginning, Jillian was easy to talk to, and no one was more fun to tease.

When I learned of auditions for the local community production of *Oklahoma!*, I felt in my bones that—in all of Indiana—no native-born son could ever embody the true spirit and ethos of an Oklahoman from centuries past as I. Indeed, my parents grew up in Oklahoma and for holidays and summer vacations, I was always staying on my grandparents' cattle farm in Eastern OK. I knew the mannerisms, I knew the syntax and expressions of its people. So, when the acting director, Kensington, asked me to audition I said, "NO THANK YOU," because it was a MUSICAL, and I am not a singer. While I had been in non-musical plays before with professional New York actors, I had no formal vocal training.

But Kensington was insistent as there was always need for more men in these local musicals, so I found myself as a supporting character with a dozen or so generic lines. I was inhabiting my role of the federal marshal as only an ACTOR would: giving myself a refined, complex, densely elaborate, intellectually satisfying backstory. Toward the finale number, I ad-libbed a line midperformance, speaking quietly, with intensity and great scorn to Laurey (Jillian). Looking into her eyes with the full fury of self-righteous indignation, I whispered, "Congratulations," upset that I

145

wasn't able to lay down the law and deliver swift justice as the acting deputy. She laughed, and—though I could tell she was breaking character—it was a joyous moment onstage, so the audience wouldn't have noticed. This was the first time I directly interacted with Jillian, and I appreciated that, even in this brief moment, she seemed to understand my humour and the inside joke.

From there, we continued the whispering of adlibs to each other onstage and moved right along to me "borrowing" her phone while she left the room during rehearsal to take selfies she would inevitably find later while I feigned ignorance; she quickly became my best friend. Once, when she asked what book I was reading while on a break during rehearsal, I pontificated for a good ten minutes, summarizing what I read ... the earnest and sincere attention she gave me with her clear blue eyes and naturally blonde hair; my heart swooned. There are only so many people on Earth that would put up with going over the fascinating (to me) things I was reading from history to biographical, near-death experiences to 'The Count of Monte Cristo'.

Jillian thought I was funny at first ... before she figured out my humour and started getting migraines from rolling her eyes so much into her head. While one of the most attentive listeners I'd met, I did find her a lot of times in a depressive state early on and only later learned how much Lithium she was on and that it acted as a wet blanket on her emotions. It isn't that she was always frowning, yet she also wasn't always smiling. She had Resting Listless Face.

It was probably the gargantuan strength and enormous cleverness of my humour that broke through and forced her to giggle at me.

On one of our early dates, while driving her to what I hoped was the perfect blend of romantic yet inexpensive dinners, she mentioned that she had stopped taking her medications and if she started hearing voices that she apologized in advance. Ignoring the cold lead in the pit of my stomach, I figured I would cross that bridge when I came to it. But as I continued to date her, she never heard any voices, and as the months (then years) passed, all her stories of the beforetime seemed a fluke ...

CHAPTER EIGHT

And now, for a lighter change of pace, it's time for a brief interlude on *How I Met My Husband.*

I knew nothing about Jeff before I encountered him at rehearsals. And we didn't have much interaction during the run of *Oklahoma!*

But I did walk away with a couple of charming stories from that time.

Before auditioning for the show, my family already had a vacation to Florida planned. My youngest sister, Jourdan, spent a great deal of our time away helping me memorize lines, and she knew my lines better than I did by the end of the trip, I'm certain.

But I missed out on any kind of introductions to the cast until they already had a week or so of rehearsals under their belts, so I didn't have much time to formally meet anyone before diving into the material.

First impressions can be very important. I was relying on perception alone, given that I wasn't properly introduced to practically anyone else in the cast. My first impression of Jeffrey was that he was a father and also a stoner.

And I was not even close. On either count.

Lesson learned. Don't judge a book by its cover and all that.

See, Jeff liked to wear a shirt that had a cow on it with a speech bubble saying "I ♥ Grass". I mean, what would *you* think? Because *I* most definitely assumed, between that and his affable charm/goofiness, it meant he partook in some illicit substances.

Naturally, it was later explained to me by the wearer himself that he lived in New York for a time and worked at a restaurant called "Bareburger" that *served grass-fed beef*. He doesn't smoke—or even drink—any illicit substances whatsoever.

Whoops.

How did I think he was a father you ask?

While I was in Florida with my *actual* family, the cast was split into "families" of its own, as in STAGE families. It was determined that a young girl, Olivia, was Jeff's "daughter".

When I finally realized she wasn't his ACTUAL daughter, I was beside myself with giggles.

Yeah, I took my time disclosing that to him.

During *Oklahoma!* we had only one direct exchange. Toward the very end of the show's run, the cast tradition was to nominate an actor to receive the "Tony". Jeff asked me how to spell my last name, and I was touched that he was voting for me.

He made sure I saw him erase it, maybe 10 seconds after he wrote it.

True love.

Hey, his first impression of me was also a complete train wreck. He thought I was a snooty, shallow moron … those may not be his exact words, but I do think the word "vapid" came up. Therefore, not splitting hairs here, he thought I was an empty void from head to toe. It wasn't until he realized I enjoyed reading—notably *The Count of Monte Cristo*—that he had any interest beyond "This is someone I like to annoy."

In other words, he didn't know I could read. Beyond a script.

And he didn't learn this tidbit until our second show together, *Arsenic & Old Lace*. With a much smaller cast and far less to-do than a musical entails, we had exceedingly more time to chat and get to know one another.

We began officially dating in October 2015. Our first date was something out of a movie.

We went to Denny's, and this smooth operator brought with him a news article from the New York Times entitled "The 36 Questions That Lead To Love".

To his credit, they did.

There were some snags along the way. I called things off a couple of times in 2016 before I was ready to be all-in. It isn't an excuse, but I was still drowning in a sea of trauma and there was some serious work to be done; it didn't seem fair to me to drag Jeff along through that hellacious roller coaster. I was constantly wracked with guilt, knowing that he was signing up to spend his life with a broken individual like myself. Much like a shattered mirror, there were fragments scattered all around, some so tiny they could hardly be seen. And though he would gladly help collect remnants without a second thought, it was something I felt I needed to do alone. And either I would return to him whole, or I wouldn't return.

I have learned many a thing from Jeffrey. Patience and total faith, for starters. Understanding and nurturing. Complete and selfless love.

And all before we even said, "I do". That didn't happen until much later.

In the meantime, we worked in several more community theatre productions. Sometimes on our own, sometimes together.

In 2017, we reunited. And I asked him if he'd move to Los Angeles with me.

KENSINGTON
(DIRECTOR/FRIEND)

I'm privileged to know Jillian in several capacities: as a director/actor, artistic team member, friend, and sometimes babysitter for my daughter (I think our relationship even developed in that order). I'm a huge fan of Jillian's voice, whether it's spoken, written or singing. She is a keen judge of character and a fiercely loyal confidant. As opposite as our personalities may be (I feel like we have a real Glinda/Elphaba vibe—from the musical *Wicked* if you're unfamiliar—going on), our friendship and working relationships have been a source of joy for me.

I like to think that Jillian asked me to contribute to her book because she loves me oh-so-very-much. That inviting my participation is like her holding me tight in the way that just screams "LOVE." I like to think all of these things because Jillian typically rolls her eyes and goes limp when I crush her with my hugs, as she is one of my favorite people, and I feel like joining her in this creative endeavor is the written version of her saying "I love you, buddy."

Well, I love you too, boo boo.

I've been a Jillian-fan since I first saw her on stage during the summer of 2015. I was the Interim Artistic Director for the Evansville Civic Theatre and, with a very small amount of notice, needed to cast the musical *Oklahoma!* for our summer production. For those of you living under a musical rock, *Oklahoma!* is one of those shows that everyone and their grandmother knows and (often) loves, and it calls for a huge cast. Off the top of my head, I couldn't think of anyone who could sing the female lead, so my fingers were crossed for new faces to turn up at auditions.

Along came Jillian.

She stood out with her stark blonde hair, quiet demeanor, and big, soprano voice. As soon as she began singing I knew I had my Laurey. Rehearsals would start soon- she was going on vacation, so I wouldn't see her for a few weeks, but I felt certain that she was going to be a wonderful addition to a cast of people with whom I'd worked in the past.

Before I delve into what it was like to work with Jillian and witness her blossoming romance with Jeffrey, I have to take an important detour. I didn't know it was important at the time, but it's worth mentioning now.

Before rehearsals began and after the cast list was posted, I went to an annual doctor's appointment. As I was leaving the appointment, one of the doctors in the office who was also a mutual friend asked to speak to me for a moment. We stepped into an office and she said, "Did you just cast Jillian Weinzapfel as the lead in your show?" I said I had. She looked thoughtful for a moment and said, "It might be a good idea to have an understudy." I waited for a beat for her to explain and when she didn't, I asked if there was something I needed to know. She said no, just that Jillian was going through some things, and I might need to be prepared with a backup. Just in case.

I did not inquire further, or understand what she could mean by that. Having read Jillian's book, I now know that this show wasn't too long after her first hospitalization. But in 2015, I was grateful to have a female lead with a degree in theatre, and especially one with clear vocal training and a quietly professional attitude. I wasn't going to look any further into the conversation unless I had a reason to. I never mentioned this conversation to Jillian or anyone else, until now.

Rehearsals were held in a local church, and our cast of less than 20 (I still don't know how we did *Oklahoma!* with less than twenty people, but we did and it was awesome.) spent their summer learning choreography and singing their hearts out. As with any community theatre production, there was a lot of socializing amongst the cast and backstage shenanigans. (I'm not typically privy to the nonsense, as actors are usually on their best behavior when I'm around. But I see it from the sidelines- community theatre can be a great way to make friends.) Jillian, however, treated her role and performance like any of the actors I worked with professionally. She was always focused, asking questions or sharing ideas about her character- she was on her A-game all the time. Even when we had to cast her romantic counterpart as a high-school-aged performer (a very talented one, mind you, but he was much younger than her), she was always doing her best. I vividly remember her professionalism.

This is the first show she did with Jeffrey, and I would be remiss not to share my most vivid memory of Jeff from *Oklahoma!*. I went to college with him, so I'm familiar with Jeff's personality and particular brand of nonsense. Helluva actor and guy, AND often a delightful pain in my butt during a show. But I digress.

My most vivid memory of Jeffrey is when he created his own intentional/unintentional dance solo on stage. During part of one of the big dance numbers, everyone was partnered up and do-si-do'ing around the stage. Except for Jeff, who went to the only part of the stage that was unoccupied by actors (inside of a bare-bones barn structure) and galloped around in circles. I caught him doing it during tech week and thought most people wouldn't notice it, and let him keep it in the show. It became a cast and crew favorite, with people asking to come sit in the loft with me so they could get the best view of his big moment. This memory is an excellent depiction of who Jeff is as a person-he emanates a child-like wonder that is strangely appealing. You can't help but love him. I would never have guessed that Jeff and Jillian would hit it off, but I'm a big fan of surprises. Life definitely surprised me with these two.

As *Oklahoma!* came to an end, we began two plays: *Arsenic and Old Lace* and *Memory of Water*. Jillian and Jeffrey were involved with both shows, as well as our friend Matt (the one that contributed to this book. Hi Matt! Love and miss you!). I noticed that Jillian was spending most of her backstage time with Jeff and Matt, and saw a slightly different version of her personality— Still the professional on stage, but more laughter and joking in the dressing room. I could see that she was making friends backstage that even extended into having conversations late into the evening in the parking lot. I was glad to witness one of my favorite parts of theatre, when people become close during a rehearsal process.

The final show we did together at the Civic was the musical *9 to 5*. This show was a wild ride on and off stage, but I'll save you some time and share my favorite Jillian moment. Her character was supposed to point a gun (stage firearm) at another character during a pivotal moment in the show and fire it (missing the guy, but it's a big laugh for the audience). I was backstage during the show listening to the action onstage, and when it got to that moment the gun didn't fire ... but the audience laughed. When I asked her what happened after the scene, she told me when she pulled the trigger the gun didn't fire the blank like it was supposed to, so she panicked and did the only thing she could think of- she threw the gun at her scene partner.

The audience loved it. I'm still tickled pink about it. Her scene partner was not a fan.

In the 2016-2017 season of shows, I was directing for my own theatre company, Think Pink Productions. Jillian and Jeffrey were vital parts of the show season, working onstage, backstage, in tech, artistic and box office positions. That was a magical year of theatre because I got to witness my friends show off their incredible talents. Jillian choreographed, performed, ran tech, the box office- she was anywhere the production (and I) needed her to be. Her talent and dedication was enormous. And Jeffrey was right alongside, running lights, performing, and bringing his delightful Jeffrey-ness to the space.

Our working relationship became more of a friendship, and I got to know Jillian more personally. She had and has a deeply caring heart, and her ability to judge someone's character is much keener than my own. She sees people for who they are right away. A beautiful part of our friendship is that, when she would know someone was bad news, she would advise me and then give me space to let everything play out. I don't think she's been wrong yet. Her quiet personality (Until you get to know her, that is … she has plenty to say after that.) and observant demeanor made her the target of unkindness from others in the theatre community. Jillian was observed as judgmental and rude, an observation that couldn't be more off base. Through all of that, she was poised and professional- always.

And she never required an understudy.

CHAPTER NINE

I had so much gushing to do about meeting my husband (It could really be its own book.) that I skipped quite a bit.

For instance, throughout 2015 (and beyond), I was still under the impression I was not REALLY bipolar. I was just going along with what the doctors said, with the intention that—so long as I did—I was not going to be admitted to another hospital.

During the run of *Arsenic & Old Lace*, I became very close friends with another cast member, Matt. I don't recall how the conversations started, but I began telling Matt all about my hospitalizations and what I went through in recent history. We would sit in my car in the theatre parking lot, sometimes until 3 in the morning, and he would simply listen as I would pour out everything I was constantly holding inside. He was an excellent friend and listener, and I'll never be able to repay the debt.

Of course, the time we spent together became the subject of rumors from some small minds in the local theatre community. Jeff was warned *prior to our first date* that I was intimately involved with Matt, who is a married man. A despicable falsehood through and through. (Just another lesson I learned from Jeff. Trust. He thanked those spreading rumors for the heads up and proceeded to ignore them completely.)

My talks with Matt eventually led me to the conclusion that the Lithium was unnecessary. At the time, it didn't seem incorrect. And being misdiagnosed certainly held its own weight in this decision. If doctors could be wrong about a schizophrenia diagnosis, then they could absolutely be wrong about a bipolar diagnosis. And hearing, "I don't think you're crazy, I really don't," from Matt was more than enough for me.

I went to see Dr. A _ _ _ around the start of the new year, 2016, after being off the Lithium for a handful of months and telling no one (except Matt and Jeff). Our appointments were fairly typical: he would ask questions about how I was doing, what was new, he would ask how the medicine was going, he'd prescribe me more, I'd be on my way. End.

I was hoping this appointment would follow the formula. It'd be too easy for him to ask about the medicine first and immediately judge everything following through a bias.

Luckily, Dr. A _ _ _ is nothing if not consistent.

He asked how I was doing and was very excited about how remarkably well I seemed. Very clear, very focused, very quick-witted. He was not ready for my answer about how my medication was going:

"I stopped taking it two months ago."

I was fired.

He was not unkind about it. He simply said there was no reason for me to continue seeing him if I wasn't going to be taking medication.

Fair enough.

Dr. A _ _ _ and my mother expressed concerns in my appointment that if things became too hectic or something caught me off guard emotionally, I would slip right back into an episode. But my sanity remained intact even though life was surprisingly full of adventure.

You see, fortunately for me, my bipolar disorder is not a constant cycling of ups and downs. If you recall from earlier chapters, I spent the next five-plus years not taking Lithium with zero incidents.

For starters, not terribly long after that very appointment, I moved into my own apartment for the first time and began teaching classes at the dance school I'd attended throughout my own childhood. This was in addition to the job I was working at Montessori and the shows I was performing in with Evansville Civic Theatre.

Emboldened by my other successful voyages back into normalcy, I attended a big audition conference—UPTAs, which stands for Unified Professional Theatre Auditions—in Memphis, Tennessee, to try and land some more theatrical contracts.

As a result of the audition, I was invited—on two separate occasions—to New York City to audition for some touring productions (An American national tour of *Annie* and an international tour of *The Wizard of Oz* taking place in Southeast Asia). If you think these undertakings weren't accompanied by off-the-chart levels of sheer panic, you are one hundo percent incorrect. I wasn't chosen for either show, but it was a VERY big deal to have been requested to audition, especially for me—the young, bipolar woman who not long ago assumed she'd seen her last stage.

At the audition for *Annie,* while we were waiting to try and wow the casting directors, I got a real kick out of another auditioner asking me if I had representation (e.g. an agent or manager). She couldn't put together how some random from Indiana was requested to attend the same audition as her.

If only she knew.

I decided sometime during the course of 2016 that I wanted to be able to put away some money in savings, so I had absorbed and was working, I think 5 jobs simultaneously? I was still working at Montessori, but—in order to begin saving more funds—I also began cleaning my grandmother's house weekly, tutoring/chauffeuring a middle school student, teaching at a different dance school, and working a couple of personal assisting jobs (Neither of which worked out. Personal Assisting gigs can get into very *WEIRD* territories.). I was also choreographing and participating in shows with Think Pink Productions. I had a *lot* on my plate.

And still no mania.

In 2017, I was able to leave my job at Montessori (and all the other jobs, too) and begin nannying for a pair of students I met while working there. That family more or less funded my move to Los Angeles and even took me out of the country for the first time.

What's a mental illness journey without a little *Eat, Pray, Love* chapter, right?

I went with the family to the Canary Islands (the island known as Tenerife) and to Madrid, Spain. It was magical. I love the Thacker family dearly, and they were instrumental to my recovery and trek out to California.

In the summer of 2017, I reunited with Jeff. He wasn't immediately on board, and I don't blame him at all. I know it wasn't emotionally an easy ask of him after I chose to call things off more than once. I had to put in some work to earn his trust back, and I did my damnedest to be deserving of a third (and final) chance.

Life seemed so busy but beautifully normal to me, and I was able to accomplish so many things I never expected to be capable of doing after the prior hospitalizations. I was having adventure after adventure, and, finally back with the person I loved and convinced I could take on the world, I decided it was time to really pursue my acting dream. I knew Jeff was ready to get out of Indiana and make it happen as much as I was.

On New Year's Day of 2018, Jeff and I made a formal announcement that we would be moving to Los Angeles. We would be pursuing our acting dreams in the land of broken dreams, film, and television.

Hollywood.

MATT (FRIEND/CASTMATE)

Arsenic & Old Lace, somehow, is now years ago, so I apologize if my memory is not 100% either.

But I do recall a moment where I shared with Jillian something one of my professors really drove home for me, which is this:

Anyone diagnosed with a mental health disorder is labeled as "crazy," and that's a very unfair characterization. To compound that, they are also then labeled AS their diagnosis instead of HAVING a diagnosis.

If someone breaks their leg, they're still "Jim, who has a broken leg."

Whereas if someone is diagnosed with schizophrenia, they are suddenly "Schizophrenic Jim."

We never say, "Oh, there goes broke-leg Jim hobbling along. Poor thing will always be that way, and that's just the way it is."

But for some reason we do that with mental health.

What I recall saying to Jillian is something along the lines of,

> "No matter what a doctor diagnoses you with, you aren't that label. You're still Jillian. You'll always be Jillian. If you break a leg, you're Jillian – who

has a broken leg. If you are diagnosed with bipolar disorder, you're still Jillian – who has bipolar."

I, of course, didn't intend to make her believe that I didn't think she had anything that the doctors said she had. My main hope at the time was that she would work on not internalizing when other people called her crazy. I vaguely recall her being bothered (as anyone would be) by the fact that it seemed people treated her differently and she just wanted to be her old self.

((And I—as any bipolar person will—took that sliver of validation of normalcy and ran with it. Not my best idea to immediately hop off the medication train; however, on the plus side, I discovered I could go YEARS without having an episode, medication or no. So, though it wasn't Matt's intention, he did help lay the foundation for some important diagnostical groundwork. I call that a win-win, Matt. And thanks for unwittingly becoming my therapist back in the day. I owe you several times over.))

CHAPTER TEN

Before moving to Los Angeles, I submitted a total of 86 job applications online. I could count on one hand how many I received follow-up calls and emails from.

Tough crowd.

We had quite the adventure before the move trying to land housing as well. Jeff and I took a cross-country, 30-hour road trip in April 2018 to apartment search, and we looked far and wide to find anything that was remotely within our price range, not a dirty closet, and also pet-friendly (for our dog, Kirby). Definitely easier said than done.

On our way back to Indiana and set to move in a month, we had nothing lined up. Things were looking grim, and we were both feeling the anxiety and panic creep in. I finally managed, after frantic Facebook searching, to find a young couple looking for new roommates to take over one of the rooms in their apartment in Koreatown, who were willing to accept couples and dogs (as they were also a couple with a dog).

Hallelujah.

Now we could move in with perfect strangers. (Side note, I wanted to add a blurb that our roommates were incredible, and we love them dearly. We really lucked out finding such awesome people and not serial killers. Thank you, Katie and Colby!)

I also received a call from a temp agency, as we were still making our way back to Indiana, and was offered a job to be sent out as a receptionist to various offices on temporary assignments.

The move—now complete with employment and housing on the horizon—was going to be far more seamless.

Once in LA, Jeff and I joined Central Casting per the suggestion of a college friend familiar with the film industry, and we began working as extras, or—as they're referred to in Hollywood— "background artists". Sometimes we'd be on set upwards of 10 hours a day. Sometimes all through the night.

I remember my first call was a night call, though it wasn't explicitly stated, and I was already set to be working the next morning at 6 a.m. for a temp assignment.

Occasionally lessons are learned the hard way.

I know I felt buzzed, but even that didn't result in a manic episode. I returned to our apartment and slept practically the rest of that day.

Money was tight, and I decided to pick up another job. I managed to find a family to nanny for, and I began doing that four days a week in addition to the sprinkling of temp jobs, background calls, and the various acting/modeling projects, auditions, and classes that I would find to attend of my own accord.

After moving into our own apartment, Jeff picked up a new job at a gas station and decided to join a listing agency. I later joined as well after seeing how positive the experience was for him. LA Casting was similar to Central Casting, but with a more personal, intimate, and exclusive feel. Whereas Central was a free service that would book hundreds and hundreds of actors no matter what (Many an ex-con gets work this way, and that's not an exaggeration.), LA Casting was a paid service that was more specific and focused; they didn't hire on just anyone, and their jobs were more in tune with the needs of the casting directors. We were able to land some really neat gigs with their help. Some even resulted in Union vouchers, helping propel our careers further toward becoming legitimate industry professionals. They were baby steps, but they were important, foundational steps to take.

Chapter Ten

In November of 2018, Jeff proposed, and I accepted. He took me to a Quiznos to commemorate the moment, with the intention of formally breaking the hex my youngest brother, Jonah, had placed upon me years before. Long story as short as I can possibly make it, when I was around 16 years old, I was waiting in line with Jonah (7, at the time) to order sandwiches at Quiznos. I felt Jonah's eyes just staring at me, the look on his face deep in thought. When I asked him what he was looking at, he—very loudly, I might add—asked, "Are you EVER going to get married?" The other customers standing around tittered, and I could feel my face burning. It's been a running joke ever since that Jonah set a curse on me that day, one that would only end if I was able to convince some poor bastard to marry me.

… sorry Jeff.

It wasn't until Jeff and I were at a Chipotle one day in 2019, enjoying one of our frequent burrito bowl trips, that we set a date for the following year. I made a joke about how it would be clever to be married in 2020 because if anyone asked when we were married, we could say, "Well in hindsight, it was 2020." When I found out October 10th was a Saturday, it was game, set, and match. 10/10/2020 was just too easy to remember. The calendar was marked and wedding planning began.

Los Angeles was a dream come true for Jeff and me as far as our acting careers were concerned. We immersed ourselves in as many experiences as we could. We could be found on many a film set, and, though we were mainly in the background, we had an inestimable number of adventures filling each and every day.

We have stories galore of our time in L.A. (Again, could be its own book.), and—had the Covid-19 pandemic not swooped in to jeopardize everything—I imagine we'd still be there.

Alas.

All good things must come to an end.

By 2020, Jeff had worked so hard that—after only two years of pure magic—he became SAG-Eligible and was able to join the SAG Union while we were in quarantine. (SAG stands for Screen Actors Guild. If you want to know more about it, that's the term you'll want to search.)

As for myself, maybe a week before quarantines were set in place, I was able to sign on with a commercial agent. It was a HUGE deal to have representation. My agent sent me on a grand total of one audition.

And then lockdowns.

And *then* crazy.

I hung in there for a little beyond half of 2020. I highly doubt I would have managed to do that on my own, had I been without the help of the family I nannied for who allowed me to continue working. I certainly have the Halaris family to thank profusely for deeming me "essential".

But eventually, those "4th of July" fireworks (In Los Angeles, they take place from May to September.) and being trapped inside (in Panorama City, of all places) really did me in.

Oh yeah, and the weed. Don't do drugs, kids. Even once a week is enough to derail your life. (To my credit, I didn't go out and purchase it. I've yet to spend a dime on marijuana. Someone else made the purchase and then, since they were from a state where it was illegal, decided to bestow it upon me.) I shouldn't have smoked, but after 5+ years of normal life, I was operating under the assumption that my diagnosis was still incorrect.

As it goes with manic episodes, I remember it in hazy tableaus.

It started with several nights of gradually less and less sleep. Fireworks were keeping our dog, Kirby, up, which in turn was keeping me up.

I was also becoming absorbed in social media. What else *was* there during quarantine, right? Twitter, Facebook, Instagram all became a daily routine for me. Once the Jeffrey Epstein story broke, I was becoming entrenched in researching conspiracy theories and things that normally I would roll my eyes at and scroll right past.

Wild ideas began taking root, and I was completely gob-smacked by them during my sudden episode. I was unaware of how firm a grip they had on my brain until well after treatment. During my episode, I was spouting insanities that would never have consumed me … if I was prepared to be on the lookout for mania.

To my chagrin, I was not at all prepared and decided to take these wild thoughts to whoever would listen to them. Why not have an encore performance of alienating friends?

There was a night of zero sleep—July 4th itself—when I was scrolling furiously about the Epstein scandal and various speculations, when suddenly an orange glow didn't fade like the others had from the corner of my vision.

I looked out the window at a palm tree ablaze right outside of our apartment complex.

I didn't come back to sanity after that night.

Jeff recognized there was a stark change in me, but he was as prepared as I was on how to handle the ensuing manic episode … which is to say, practically not at all. And understandably so—neither one of us at this point truly thought I was bipolar. Remember, this is a full, incident-and-medication-free, 5+ years from my first episode, with nary a mood swing in between. That was a dark and distant memory floating in the ocean of my past.

We were brutally unprepared for the present-day tsunami.

He began feverishly calling my family members, doctors, my medical insurance reps, looking anywhere and everywhere for someone to help me.

He didn't want to take me to the hospital. He knew how much it would destroy me. Worse still, our relationship.

After being met with "We aren't accepting new patients" from several doctors' offices, thanks to the pandemic and lockdowns, he knew options were bleakly limited.

In the meantime, I was destroying my life for a second spell. The state of our apartment became a reflection of how my brain was working. As in, it was in absolute turmoil, unforgiving disarray. I was making Jeff, Kirby, my employers, my family, my friends, all nervous wrecks. Through no control of my own. I was sinking into psychosis, and there was no coming out of it without medical intervention.

Jeff knew it. And somewhere waaaaaaaaay down deep inside, I must've known it, too. Because I let him convince me to go to the hospital.

Round 2.

JENNA (YOUNGER SISTER/ PSYCH NURSE)

Jillian and Jeff were **_DOING the damn thing._**
They are out in California and I must say, KILLIN'
it. I was bragging about them every chance I got.
I mean, how cool is it to see your own sister in a
"Superstore" season finale episode, with America
Ferrera right there? MY SISTER, sprinkled throughout
Season One of "The L Word Generation Q" or walking across a set of the season premiere episode of
"The Fix," with a story to tell about briefly speaking with Scott Cohen (from Gilmore Girls). Or, to
know that they are working together as extras on
a super well-known franchise in the horror genre,
and I wasn't even allowed to know exactly what
it was (Non-disclosure agreements are the worst).
    Back in Indiana, as a trained psych nurse in my
third year at this point, I saw the effects of Covid
in very real time. With increased isolation and de-
creased productivity comes depression, anxiety,
and feeling generally bleh. Mass chaos ensued
across the nation and mental health issues flared
up (and continue to) while social media fueled
the fire. Now, with an audience almost forced to

stay connected virtually, people were constantly engaged online, as there wasn't much else they could do. There was little regard for validity of information, just rapidly absorbing and regurgitating it, everyone seemingly-stuck in a vicious cycle. Paranoia was at an ALL-TIME high. With the pandemic center stage, the skepticism for medical professionals increased among all patients.

In my field, this is already an everyday battle.

To recap and add a little to my own story: I graduated with my Bachelors in the Science of Nursing and knew I wanted to do one of two fields—psychiatry or pediatrics. Now, I had always wanted to do pediatrics; working with kids had been part of my plan since I was a wee one myself. But I had never really considered psychiatry until that experience with Jillian's first episode years prior. It left an impact on me. I had a few clinical rotations in some psych facilities around the community that made me realize what I had gained through that tumultuous time period. I had an understanding that some could not develop through schooling. Watching someone you care about go through something most cannot fathom gives you such deep empathy for the patients and families experiencing the same hopelessness you've felt. It draws you in to reassure them in any way possible that you have seen people in this spot before, and they absolutely can get better. It also aids in giving you immense amounts of resilience and patience to deal with whatever those you are caring for might throw at you (literally or metaphorically). I have my sister to thank for my passion and career. When I am having a rough day, I remember that it could be my family member as much as anyone's and I make **damn** sure I treat that person how I would want a member of my family treated.

Alrighty. That said, back to California:

It is July 12th, 2020, when I text my mother to express my concern. I simply state "I'm worried about Jillian." This concern was brought about because she had been posting rather long, frequent posts on Facebook in video form. Already out of character for her, as she is mostly a private person. Add to that, her rapid, pressured speech with no time to even take a breath, jumping from topic to topic (strange subject matters, too) with seeming association in her mind (aka loose associations), and her disheveled appearance, which all struck me that much harder.

There was also the look in her eye. One that I recognized instantly, as I had seen it before in her, years prior. And one that I had come to notice in many of my patients when they are acutely psychotic. It took a little time for me to come up with the best way to describe it: picture a fixed gaze, yet there is a distinct blankness behind it. It is like they are looking at you so intensely, but also looking right through you because they are actually miles away. And in Jillian's particular case, her pupils become so constricted, they would be described as "pinpoint" in medical jargon.

Many of us in the family were already on the same page with this concern due to individual and group conversations with Jillian. My mom contacted Jeff to inquire about her, as he had not yet experienced this firsthand and may not know what is to come or how to handle it. He mentioned her sleep routine had become disrupted and that she had decided to call off work until she "receives a sign that things are okay to be there." With this, I could tell that she knew, she could feel something was not right, something was off. She couldn't exactly express it, but she had enough lucidity to KNOW that she was not well enough to continue working. She loved her job at the time, nannying an adorable set of young brothers.

Then, another message my mother sent. From Jillian herself:

> "I'm waiting for a sign. And I believe that God or the Universe will give it to me."

I was thrown off completely by this. Needing further verification, I asked Mom directly,

> "She sent you that?"

> "Yes."

This was such an out-of-place thing for Jillian to say. Now, if my sister had always been much into religion, I may not have thought anything of it. But, knowing her, I simply replied,

> "She needs to be seen, go in somewhere."

My mother also mentioned that Jillian had cried three times in their last five conversations, had not been eating due to saying she "just doesn't feel hungry," but tried to reassure me that she still had some lucidity, so it was not yet complete. I again stated my opinion,

"She still needs to be seen."

Now, my mother is a much stronger and more patient woman than I. This, she and I have established many a time.

At this point, I am ready to board the next flight out and get Jillian over to the first place I find. It's happening again. And here I am, over 2,000 miles away. Over a day to drive there. This time, trained in this field and understand enough to maybe help, yet helpless again. The voice of reason and ever so calm, mom said she simply let Jeff know that she believes Jillian is "sliding" and that she is "in trouble in her opinion."

From here, she informs me she plans to let Jeff take the lead.

I immediately realize I have severe control issues because I am thinking, *No absolute freakin' way could I do that, whether she's grown and about to be married or not!* Not that Jeff is not perfectly capable and the absolute best person to be leading the way with Jillian. I just don't know if I could've had the same gumption as Mom to 'let go' of the control in her shoes.

Jeff and my mom conversed, and he brought up the word "manic." This seems small but was of great relief to me because I was not sure how much Jillian and Jeff had discussed about her past regarding mental health. I also did not know whether Jillian had ever believed mania was truly a possibility. In part, due to the last roller coaster of treatment, followed by such a long period of time that she had been off medication with no sign of illness returning. Jeff also said Jillian had mentioned seeing a therapist not too long ago, so he planned to use that as "an in" to see if he could get her to see someone. My mom forwarded a list from NAMI of psychiatrists and the mental health crisis guide for the area. We were skeptical she would willingly seek treatment based on her last experience, yet still trying to be hopeful that if she can see someone before she is completely severed from reality, it will be easier this time.

There were a few factors that could've played a part or compounded this particular spiral for Jillian. First, the sudden stop of life as we all knew it with the pandemic. Second, being out in California and living in a somewhat not-so-great area while having a small support system that is not immediately available, with the exception of Jeff. Third, she had stopped her medication long ago. To be fair, who could be sure it was needed? It had been literal years since any issue occurred that indicated the need of medicine. Not to mention, after the experiences of the previous hospitalizations, the confidence of them being correct wasn't exactly soaring. Fourth, she had begun to dip back into smoking THC. Fifth, the state of the nation seemed bleak and only appeared to worsen every day as scandal after scandal occurred like rapid fire. And, lastly, as Jillian has mentioned before, research shows late summer being known to show a spike in relation to mania/manic behavior.

But there is also more awareness this time among all of us. Maybe, just maybe, we have a chance to catch this runaway train.

July 13th, I text Jillian myself just to get my own feel of the situation (again, control issues, I know). I start out simple, asking what she has done today. She states she made a Facebook Live, calling out one of the facilities in our hometown. In the state of mind she is in, she is not considering how this may affect the psych-nurse-sister working at said facility. My heart drops as I ask cautiously (but knowing I won't like the answer),

"About what?"

"My story. Your story. Our story."

She of course means well but mentions me directly and that they 'work me to death.' Ever the outspoken one, ready to battle for her siblings, she goes on to state I have an ENORMOUS heart and they are taking advantage of it. She states,

"You've been afraid to ask for help, but I've seen you. I've heard you. I've watched you be taken advantage of. I will not let them hurt you anymore. No. More. I love you."

Of course, feeling mortified (and obviously wanting to keep my job), I ask her to delete it. I try not to let myself become upset that she did not

180

obtain my consent, but I can't help being a bit miffed. I do tell her that she is more than welcome to tell HER story but to please leave me out of it. She is insistent,

> "It's the same story, I have to tell the whole story. Don't you see it? You're Anna and I'm Elsa."

I forward these screenshots to my mother, at a loss.

Get me out to California, STAT.

The morning of July 14th, I received a long text from my mother. This time, it is a forwarded text from my Aunt Britt, who just spent quite some time conversing with Jillian via phone. She explains that when Jillian talks about people she loves, her siblings, the boys she babysits, Kirby, she is extremely lucid. Other moments, she talks about books, musicals, lyrics, and it was lost on Aunt Britt. Jillian reported at this time she had slept for a few hours the night before but could not remember her last shower. She reported she was "fasting" as humans are "mostly water." Aunt Britt was able to get her to eat a banana while speaking with her. Jillian also reported to Aunt Britt she had informed the couple she nannied for that she was showing signs of COVID, which was why she was unable to work at the moment. When Britt asked why she had told them that, she said she was "worried," but didn't explain any further. Again, we surmise that she seems to know SOMETHING is off but she cannot quite express what. They stayed on the line until

Jeff arrived home and Aunt Britt spoke with him briefly.

After yesterday's conversation and this morning's report, I am really ready to fly out. **What are we waiting for?** I am trying to make plans with my mother, stating,

"One or two of us need to fly out."

I am suggesting I talk to my boss to get off work for the time being. I am suggesting Mom go. I am suggesting Jake could maybe go and continue to work remotely. I am suggesting Jourdan can go with one of us. All I know is, we need to be there and ready to help Jeff with what is coming. My mom suggested buying her own plane ticket and bringing Jillian back to Evansville, but this worried me, as she appeared to be in and out of reality. Putting her on a plane seemed terrifying, and her navigating layovers or even just one airport to another?

Absolutely impossible, even if someone traveled along with her.

July 14th evening, Jeff updates us. He has called around all day with referrals provided by Jillian's insurance and was FINALLY able to set up an appointment for the upcoming Friday, July 17th. He comments,

"Which seems forever."

Fortunately, this is followed by somewhat relieving news. She is beginning to sleep and eat more.

And even better, she is recognizing she needs help! He reports she does not have her regular coherence yet, so he is planning to take her into the ER if she seems to get worse before Friday. My mom asks if he is able to have someone stay with her while he works, but he has taken off through Saturday at this point.

We can breathe. Jeff is handling this, and really well at that. I can stop being so neurotic.

Afternoon of July 15th, Jeff texts my mother, disheartened again. She didn't appear to sleep at all the past night and her condition has taken a turn for the worse. He is unsure if he should take her to the ER and is asking Mom to give him a call, commenting the psychiatrist appointment seems "very far away right now."

When Mom calls me, she states she could hear Jillian "nonstop monologuing" in the background and per Jeff, she was pacing ...

JEFFREY (HUSBAND)

In late July of 2020, Jillian's mother texted me that Jillian was slipping and asked if I could call her. I'd never had a one-on-one conversation with Brooke on the phone before, and this would mark the first of a previously unanticipated many. I was currently working at my side hustle as a week-end gas station attendant, so it would have to wait until later that night. I knew that Jillian needed help, but I wasn't quite certain how and in what way. Lately, she was tirelessly, end-lessly pacing around the apartment when I was there and wouldn't sit still. She wasn't sleeping, and she was engrossed in watching these dark conspiracy YouTube documentaries all the time. I never saw her sleep anymore, and when I was slumbering and happened to wake up, there she was on her phone, scrolling through Twitter or other social media. She was convinced most celebrities drank the blood of children in order to maintain their youth and vitality. And it was so obvious the Illuminati was controlling the culture. The usual Jillian I knew (in the past 5-ish years I'd spent with her to this point) would be at the very least skeptical of these YouTube videos. And while there may be one or two celebrities that drink the blood of children, if most of them were doing it, we would have heard more about it by now. I suggested she might try taking a 24-hour break from social media, and though she'd nod in agreement, she'd immediately resume tumbling down her rabbit hole of conspiracy videos. I kept hoping and wishing that Jillian would GO TO SLEEP. In my estimation, if she could only get a good night's rest, a lot of her restlessness and agitation would go away. I already knew from a multitude of comments she'd made previously that she wouldn't see a psychiatrist as she did not trust them, but she was reaching a point that had me hoping a psychologist/counseling session would be acceptable.

That night, as I was finally driving home from work, Brooke called and related how bizarre and "off" Jillian's conversations went lately. She had started a group chat earlier that day with her siblings and was texting a storm, and everyone could tell she wasn't being herself. Brooke was concerned and knew that I hadn't witnessed Jillian's extreme behaviour from years ago. After our call, I had a term for her behaviour: Mania.

The week before Jillian was hospitalized, I came home from work on a Sunday, and Jillian was on the phone with her aunt, Britt. She gave the phone to me, and Britt calmly explained how she had been on the phone with Jillian for ... I want to say over two hours, or a very long time at least. They tried talking about innocuous things, and Britt was clearly waiting for me to come back to the apartment before she ended the phone time. Her family and I trusted her to be alone less and less. I went to the kitchen to get some food, and Jillian followed me absentmindedly. Soon after, I moved to the bathroom and started washing my hands and brushing my teeth. Jillian followed me and looked at me with bemused eyes. She asked giddily:

"Are you following me?"

While this could be taken as a droll, tongue-in-cheek comment on her normal days, the more I talked to her, the more I realized she clearly thought I was the one following HER and that I was planning something, some big surprise. And it was going to be delightful because in this current stage of her Mania, the world was filled with fantastical things, and it was almost too much to take. Indeed, she would later become weepy and tearful at how wondrous the stars were tonight. Gone was the previous apprehensiveness and suspicion, replaced with euphoria.

On Monday, Jillian was still wandering around the apartment, but she'd entered into a strange, dreamy state of being. One moment, she would be on top of the world, gushing with excitement, and then a half an hour later she was crying over something—who knows what—and absolutely inconsolable. Almost every hour, there would be at least a minute or two where she grew to be very sad and despondent. I took Jillian and our small dog, Kirby, out for a walk in the park to try and get some fresh air, hoping that some exercise would do her good. It was an arduous process as she seemed incapable of moving at a normal pace. Normally, Jillian walked at a quick pace, and when we took walks together, I almost had to jog to keep up with her. Not today. She kept stumbling and shuffling around, so happy with the sun and the color of the grass, and the perfect stick for Kirby lying on the ground, and—even though the stick quickly snapped in half—it was made even more perfect by breaking, and how glorious it was, Life. The tears flowed.

At about midday on Monday, she was standing over the dishes in the sink that she had started thirty minutes earlier, when it dawned on her that she was still on the same piece of Tupperware she'd washed before. She kept getting distracted and coming back to the same dish, over and over, and/or forgetting she'd washed it already and grabbing it again. When it finally hit her, there was a brief moment of clarity as she grew alarmed and asked,

"What's happening to me?"

"I don't know, Jillian, let's call someone," I replied.

She assented and almost immediately there was a long, grueling process of me calling on her behalf, the numbers and redirects from her insurance card to get some sort of care. We had never needed to access healthcare in California to this point and had to rely blindly on whoever and whatever her insurance referred us to. I was able to schedule an appointment with a psychiatrist for Friday. While I had no idea at the time, I was told later that this was very quick—to have an appointment within the week. Unfortunately, Jillian was never able to make it.

By Tuesday, Jillian's condition grew even worse. I was still foolishly hoping that if she would just go to sleep then things would be fine, but she wasn't sleeping at all. She kept on moving. She kept on dancing, especially. Even when there wasn't any music. There was a music and rhythm in her head, and she kept going and going and going. Whenever I probed and asked why she was moving the pots around, or tapping on them as if listening to some deep inner mystical tone, or why she was dancing with no music playing, her mind would reach for an explanation, and—not able to express one—she would respond with, "Well … It's kind of a long story." This ended up being her default answer whenever I tried pointing out the silly things she was doing, in the hopes that she might be able to see the nonsensicalness of it with me. While in the last couple days it was hard to have a conversation with her, now it was virtually impossible. And ever since that Sunday night, I was afraid to leave her alone.

At this point Brooke, Jenna, and Jake were checking in with and messaging me. And indirectly, the rest of her family through them. I knew they had been talking to one another and texting Jillian, and they knew she was off. I was unfortunately their only contact to what was going on firsthand, though, as they were literally thousands of miles away in Indiana while we were locked down in Southern California.

I kept wishing Friday would hurry up and get here. Jillian was deteriorating by the day. We were in the height of Covid lockdowns, so I wasn't needed at work during the week. Being locked down did nothing to help Jillian's mental state, as we were always cooped up in our apartment, and she was naturally afraid to go out at night if I wasn't there. Nothing was open; there was practically nowhere to go. But at least the parks had been reopened, so I once again tried to get Jillian outside and into some fresh air. This time we went a little farther than last, to LA's reservoir. There were two things that struck me the most during this evening walk: One was that the reservoir was like a medium-sized lake with geese and fish and whatnot, and typically our dog Kirby was always kept on a tight leash. Otherwise, Jillian was afraid he would jump into the lake, and the geese would get him, and that would be the end of him. And now, suddenly she didn't care, even prompted Kirby to jump in. I couldn't trust her with the leash at all, as she would just drop it and leave Kirby to wander by himself. Jillian thought it the funniest thing, how alarmed I was. And number two, she was also saying hello to *everyone*, and my Jillian was not that friendly (in a good way). Especially to complete LA strangers. Maybe to one or two if the stars aligned, and the sun and moon eclipsed just right. However, to *every* random passerby? With a big wave and greeting?

The fresh air and exercise were not helping. She was still not sleeping, not at all. And I was feeling very beleaguered. I would catch an hour or two of sleep here and there at night, but she was still up. I had cut her off from Facebook, as the past week she kept on using Facebook live. One of our mutual friends even messaged me, "Something is wrong with Jillian, and she needs help." And while previously I had not been able to control her rants on Facebook live (or, alternatively, an endless silence, where she would be live and playing music in the background and not saying anything but keeping it on), I deleted her app Sunday, and she was not able to remember her passwords, so she was not able to Facebook live again at the height of her episode, for what it was worth.

At a certain point, loyal and ever-clingy Kirby started to avoid Jillian and back away from her. He kept lingering next to me, and not for the usual reasons of me having food. Jillian reached a point where she felt she could commune with Kirby (as well as most animals) in a metaphysical, psychic way. Except, of course, when I heard the door slam suddenly from the other room, and I noticed Kirby was nowhere to be found. I was cleaning up after her "creative cooking" in the kitchen (Manic cooking leaves much to be desired by any culinary standards). I quickly realized Jillian had let him outside our apartment. I rushed to open the door to find him clawing at it, confused why he was let out with no humans by him. I demanded to know why she did that to him and she responded in outrage, "To TRAIN him!" Jillian loves her dog, and the fact she was leaving him alone in the streets of LA impressed upon me this was not Jillian anymore. These weren't the actions of someone who was mostly Jillian but a little hyper, or a little confused, or a little paranoid. I was only away from her for a moment, even just in an adjacent room, but I couldn't possibly watch her all the time.

She was getting worse and worse, more incoherent, more dancing, more random clothes she kept dressing herself in. Since Friday couldn't come soon enough, I once again went to her insurance card to find a general practitioner we could see … perhaps get some sort of interim medication to calm her down until she could consult a psychiatrist … perhaps they could refer us even sooner to a specialist. I was shook when I called the general practitioner's office; the doctor her insurance provided her was not taking new clients "due to Covid." There was only one general practitioner that was provided for her in the system. I called again—for the ump-teenth time—a general help line and explained that Jillian needed to see a doctor, and I cannot get one scheduled for her. I spent endless hours on hold, or being redirected, or given a laundry list of other numbers to call, etc. Occasion-ally, since I was trying to schedule it for Jillian, and I was only her fiancé at this time, I would have to prompt Jillian to say, "Yes, I give permission," for me to ask these things on her behalf … which she would mumble as if I was holding her captive. I was never able to schedule a regular doctor's visit for her. The only options available seemed to be vaguely named clinics and Planned Parenthood, and I was uncertain whether these would help her at all.

By Wednesday night, she was babbling and speaking in tongues. Very much like those cliché horror movies where the person is possessed, although no levitation. I would lie in bed trying to rest and Jillian would keep nudging me, then—breaking some imaginary fourth wall on the ceil-ing—finger-point, saying in effect, "Get a load of this guy!" Again, and again, and again. I would do my best to gently move her hands away, but moments later she would poke my shoulder, look back up at the ceiling, and babble. She started doing this thing where she would breathe heavily, like she was in labor, and continue to babble. At this point, she was not physically moving from the bed to do her usual pacing, and I don't think she was capable of moving quickly while walking; however, she was still always moving in place. I'm 99.9% certain that her body—by this point—no longer even had the physical capacity required to do any more pacing. Otherwise, I assume she would be.

Her body's strength was spent, but her brain wasn't slowing down for a second.

Now de facto confined to the bed, there would be a moment of calm, and then she would gyrate and babble and sometimes say things that sounded coherent but lacked all context. It was the movements of someone who was sleepwalking and having an intense dream, so they kept moving; however, her eyes were open. All the time. Since Saturday, I do not think she had been able to sleep more than four hours TOTAL. And her mind was crashing, but she still wasn't sleeping … just engaging in a lucid dream state. Sometime between 2-4 in the morning I put on "The Adventures of Elmo in Grouchland" as a way to distract her since she could not pay attention to anything else. I tried to sleep while it was on but to no avail; I felt it was surprisingly good for a movie intended for a 5-year-old, with Elmo learning about sharing his favorite blanket, and the cast of Sesame Street defeating the selfish, envious Huxley who wanted the blanket and everything else in Grouchland. The fact that Jillian decided she knew fluent sign language and would work her hands feverishly interpreting the audio wasn't going to help me sleep either. In her own way, she was quite inventive and expressive, and she harmonized the energy and movement of her hand with the current mood and tone of the film, depending on who was speaking. Almost like a music conductor/pup-peteer. It was also all baloney, as she only knew how to say basic phrases and her alphabet in sign language and that's all. But in the wee hours, the revelation of how to use sign language sprang forth.

Looking back, I feel as if I should have just taken her to the ER Monday, but hindsight is 2020.

I was exhausted, and—although I kept mitigating the seriousness of her condition in my mind and hoping perchance a psychiatrist appointment was all we needed—I called Brooke and explained that Jillian was unintelligible now, and I felt I had no choice but to take her to the hospital. She agreed and supported my decision. Her family and I had discussed this possibility in our group message.

I think partly I knew how hurt she would be, how betrayed she would feel … especially knowing it was me that put her back into a hospital, back into a psychiatric ward … that held me back from doing so earlier. Jillian had harbored resentment for years toward anyone she felt was involved in forcing her to commit herself to the psych ward. While it's viewed "technically" as a voluntary admittance into the hospital system, it must have been obvious to anyone involved at the time that there was no free will, no rational decision-making happening, and Jillian was not capable of thinking for herself. Indeed, her admittance papers, the parts not filled out by me on this particular occasion, were unintelligible doodles of some half hieroglyphs/half Asiatic-looking script.

The local hospital in Panorama City was only a couple blocks from where we lived, so we were able to walk to it. Thankfully, I did not have to try putting her into a vehicle. I told her we were going to see a doctor. As she had been wearing the same dress for at least four days straight now in the hot LA summer, I thought I might help her into a change of day clothes. She called me a son-of-a-bitch, which made me think there may have been some sense of what was happening, but she couldn't have been too self-aware. During the walk to the hospital, she was speaking English to me the entire time and holding my hand. What she said didn't make much sense. But at least it was finally English. She told me that she was sad. I asked her, "Why?" and she replied she was, "… sad for our baby." I asked if she thought we had a baby, or did she think she was carrying, and she replied, "Both." By this point, I had learned that if I just accepted whatever she said, she would keep moving with me and letting me guide her.

The minute we stepped into the ER waiting room she spoke exclusively in what I can only describe as pig-Mandarin. This was not quite the incoherent babbling from earlier, but it certainly wasn't English. It reminded me of an episode of *Lost* where a character was knocked on the head, and she couldn't speak English but only her native Korean; however, Jillian was ignorant of any Asian dialect … not that she let it stop her. I filled out all her paperwork for her, and then she signed her name in imitation-Chinese characters. (Days later, she informed me vaguely she thought I knew she was faking, that she was doing a bit, some sort of comedy routine or long con, etc.; she had forgotten to tell me about it, that's all. I'm sure she was just embarrassed and trying to save face, though she didn't quite have the capacity to do so.) There we waited (in the lobby) for at least a half-hour before a nurse asked for Jillian. Now, because of the Covid regulations (and perhaps general California regulations?), I was not allowed past the admittance room as I was only Jillian's fiancé, but I half-barged in anyway because how in the world could they possibly diagnose, much less even process, her in her condition? She was ***incoherent.*** After some back and forth, the staff realized they did have to allow me to help. Only later did I realize I should have obtained a medical release form so the personnel working directly with Jillian could share updates on her condition with me. It was all very controlled, the processing of a new patient.

All of a sudden, in a harsh turn from the forever-long waiting and waiting I'd become accustomed to, I was saying goodbye, and that I would be outside (but close), and the most reassuring, "The doctors and nurses will take care of you now," I could muster, and then I sat back down in the waiting room ...

JACOB (OLDER BROTHER)

THE OTHER PART I CAN RECALL OF MY DIRECT IN-
VOLVEMENT WITH JILLIAN'S BIPOLAR JOURNEY WAS
A 3-HOUR PHONE CONVERSATION WE HAD WHEN
I WAS ON MY WAY BACK TO INDIANAPOLIS FROM
EVANSVILLE THAT WAS, IF I REMEMBER CORRECT-
LY, ONLY A FEW DAYS AFTER THE SECOND EPISODE
STARTED TAKING EFFECT AND MAYBE A COUPLE OF
DAYS BEFORE SHE WAS HOSPITALIZED IN CALIFOR-
NIA.

SHE HAD TEXTED ME, AND I BELIEVE I WAS THE
LAST ONE SHE TEXTED (NONE TAKEN.) BECAUSE
WHENEVER I ASKED THE REST OF OUR SIBLINGS,
THEY ALL CONFIRMED THEY ALREADY HAD THE SAME
CONVERSATION WITH HER, WITH THE EXCEPTION
OF JOSH (SINCE HE STARTED HIS MILITARY TRAIN-
ING AND DIDN'T HAVE MUCH FREE TIME TO TALK).
THE TEXT ITSELF SIMPLY ASKED IF I HAD TIME FOR
A PHONE CALL AND SOMETHING ABOUT RED PILL/
BLUE PILL.

NOW, FOR THE UNINITIATED (AND FOR GEN Z
WHO ONLY SAW THE LATEST MOVIE), THE BLUE PILL
VS RED PILL REFERENCE COMES FROM THE MATRIX
MOVIE SERIES. IN THE MOVIE, NEO, THE MAIN CHAR-
ACTER, IS OFFERED A CHOICE OF TAKING A BLUE

PILL OR A RED PILL. IF HE CHOOSES THE BLUE PILL, HE GETS TO RETURN BLISSFULLY IGNORANT TO THE REALITY OF THE MATRIX AND GO ABOUT HIS LIFE IN IGNORANCE. IF HE CHOOSES THE RED PILL, HOW-EVER, IT ACTS AS A HOMING DEVICE AND ALLOWS HIM TO BE ABLE TO BE "UNPLUGGED" FROM THE LIE THAT IS THE MATRIX. BASIC GIST, HE GETS TO KNOW THE TRUTH BUT THEN HAS TO LIVE WITH THE HARSH REALITY OF KNOWING IT. NOW, OBVIOUSLY (AND SPOILER ALERT IF YOU HAVEN'T SEEN IT), HE CHOOSES THE RED PILL; OTHERWISE THERE WOULD BE NO SERIES, AND IT WOULD BE THE MOST ANTI-CLIMACTIC MOVIE OF ALL TIME. BUT THIS IS THE QUESTION THAT SHE ASKED ME: IF I WANTED THE BLUE PILL OR IF I WANTED "TO BE RED PILLED"?

I KIND OF JUST BRUSHED IT OFF AT FIRST, AS I'M SURE ANYONE WOULD HAVE. IT SEEMED FAIRLY HARMLESS, AFTER ALL. HOWEVER, THERE WAS STILL A WARNING THAT WAS FLASHING IN THE BACK OF MY MIND. ANY HINT OF AN ILLNESS HAD BEEN "DORMANT" FOR OVER FIVE YEARS, LEADING MOST OF US TO BELIEVE THAT EVERYTHING THAT HAD HAPPENED PREVIOUSLY WAS A FLUKE AND SIMPLY WAS THE WORK OF LACED "MARY JANE," AS THE KIDS CALL IT. SEE? I'M STILL HIP TO THE LINGO! DAMN KIDS ...

SO, THE CONVERSATION STARTED WITH CONSPIR-ACY THEORIES, WHICH I CANNOT HELP BUT TO ADMIT THAT I SOMETIMES FIND FASCINATING. THE WAY SOME PEOPLE WILL CONNECT THE DOTS SOMETIMES, AND IT, AGAINST ALL ODDS, MAKES SENSE. THE FLIPSIDE BEING, OF COURSE, WHERE IT IS ... WELL, TO PUT IT POLITELY, A STRETCH THE SIZE OF THE

GIANT FROM JACK AND THE BEANSTALK WHEN HE WAS TRYING TO GET HIS GOLDEN GOOSE BACK. YOU KNOW ... IT'S A REACH. SOMETIMES THERE ARE ABSOLUTELY MASSIVE LEAPS TO CONNECT IMPROBABLE DOTS.

NEVERTHELESS, WE STARTED DOWN THE ROAD. THE FIRST THING WE TALKED ABOUT WAS EPSTEIN, AS IT WAS IN THE CURRENT NEWS CYCLE. EVEN THINKING ABOUT IT NOW, THAT PART MAKES TOTAL SENSE SINCE IT WAS, AND STILL IS, A VERY LARGE CONTROVERSY.

THEN, THINGS STARTED TO GET A LITTLE MORE SIDEWAYS. WE STARTED TALKING ABOUT HOW THE ACTORS' GUILD WAS IN CAHOOTS WITH THE GOVERNMENT, WHICH IS NOT THAT CRAZY TO THINK, I GUESS ... PEOPLE IN POWER STICK TOGETHER, RIGHT? I COULD STILL KIND OF SQUINT, TILT MY HEAD, AND CONNECT THE DOTS THERE.

AFTER THAT, THOUGH, IT REALLY TOOK OFF. I SWEAR IN THAT THREE-HOUR CONVERSATION, WE TALKED ABOUT EVERY SINGLE CONSPIRACY, FROM ALIENS TO WHETHER OR NOT MARK ANTONY WAS HELPING JULIUS CAESAR; WE COVERED IT ALL!

BUT IT WASN'T THE TOPICS OF CONVERSATION THAT TRIGGERED MY SPIDEY SENSES, IT WAS MORE THE WAY THEY WERE BEING PRESENTED.

NORMALLY, IN OUR CONVERSATIONS ON THE PHONE (WHICH I WILL ADMIT ARE FEW, AS THEY ARE WITH MOST OF OUR FAMILY ... OR AT LEAST THAT'S MY EXPERIENCE), THERE IS AT LEAST A SEMBLANCE OF STRUCTURE. OUR CONVERSATIONS ALWAYS END UP LENGTHY BECAUSE WE HAVEN'T SPOKEN TO EACH OTHER IN A WHILE AND HAVE A FAIR AMOUNT OF

CATCHING UP TO DO. NOT OUT OF ANGER OR DONE PURPOSEFULLY, WE JUST HAVE OUR OWN LIVES GOING ON. HOWEVER, NORMALLY, WHEN ONE OF US FEELS LIKE WE'RE GETTING SIDETRACKED, WE TRY TO REIN IT BACK IN. THIS WAS NOT THE CASE WITH THIS PARTICULAR PHONE CALL. IT WAS JUST TANGENTS ON TANGENTS ON TANGENTS.

ALSO, NORMALLY, IT IS MORE OF AN EQUAL SHARE OF WHO IS DOING THE TALKING. NOT THIS TIME. I COULD BARELY GET A WORD IN EDGEWISE, AND WHENEVER I DID, IT WAS HARD FOR ME TO COME UP WITH ANYTHING TO SAY. BY THE TIME THERE WAS ROOM FOR ME TO ADD ANY OF MY OWN WORDS TO THE CONVERSATION, JILLIAN HAD COVERED THREE SEPARATE TOPICS THAT WOULD BE SEEMINGLY-UNRELATED MOST OF THE TIME. THEREFORE, I JUST LET HER KEEP GOING UNTIL SHE FELT LIKE SHE HAD NOTHING ELSE TO SAY ABOUT THE MATTER.

I HAVE TURNED THIS ACTION OVER IN MY MIND A THOUSAND TIMES AT LEAST. WAS THAT THE RIGHT THING TO DO? DID I ENABLE THIS EPISODE BY DOING SO? I TRULY DO NOT KNOW THE ANSWER TO EITHER OF THOSE QUESTIONS. I WILL TELL YOU, WITHOUT A DOUBT, THE NEXT THING I DID DEFINITELY FELT LIKE THE RIGHT THING TO DO.

IMMEDIATELY AFTER WE ENDED OUR CALL, I CALLED MOM (YEAH, YEAH. CALL ME A TATTLETALE IF YOU WANT),

> "HAVE YOU HAD A CONVERSATION WITH JILLIAN LATELY? LIKE A REAL, FULL-ON CONVERSATION?"

When Mom told me she really hadn't for at least a week or two, I suggested she should give Jillian a call and see what she thought. She did, thankfully, the next day. When she called me back, I could hear the worry in her voice, but she was trying, again, to keep me from worrying, I think. She told me Jillian said that she just hadn't slept well the night before and was just tired. But that didn't sit right with me: How could she have been "so tired" and yet had enough energy just the day before to basically carry on a three-hour monologue?

I want to say that phone call was on Sunday, and by Tuesday or Wednesday things had decidedly taken a sharp turn for the worse.

Mom told me Jeff contacted her, and—while she didn't get the opportunity to speak with Jillian directly—she could hear her in the background just constantly going. Sometimes in English, sometimes in gibberish, sometimes just humming or singing, but constant. She told Jeff she was going to travel to California Friday, and she would help out in any way she could, but she could tell Jeff was very concerned and probably more than a little scared. Mom started a group conversation with Jeff, Jenna, and me all involved so that if he had any questions or needed to act sooner than Friday, he could ask away and/or keep us informed.

Now, I will admit, I did not feel like I got much of a chance to meet or get to know

JEFF BEFORE HE AND JILLIAN MOVED OUT TO LA TOGETHER. NOT THROUGH ANYONE'S FAULT, IT WAS JUST LIFE. I STARTED WORKING AT IFBI AND LIVING IN INDY, WHERE I HAD BEEN FOR 4 YEARS BY THAT POINT, WHILE THEY WERE DOWN IN EVANSVILLE, AND I DIDN'T GET TO COME HOME MUCH. I DID NOT DISLIKE JEFF BY ANY MEANS (AFTER ALL, I DIDN'T REALLY KNOW THE GUY), BUT THE WAY HE REACTED IN THIS SITUATION GARNERED HIM MORE RESPECT FROM ME THAN ANYTHING THUS FAR.

IT WAS THURSDAY, THE DAY BEFORE MOM WAS TO FLY OUT THERE, AND JEFF WAS AT HIS WIT'S END. HE FELT THAT THE ONLY OPTION WAS TO GO TO THE HOSPITAL. AND HE WAS HONESTLY RIGHT, BUT HE WAS ABSOLUTELY TORN FOR THE REASONS MENTIONED PRIOR: HE KNEW HOW MUCH SHE DID NOT WANT TO GO INTO ANOTHER HOSPITAL AND FEARED WHAT IT WOULD MEAN FOR HER. HOWEVER (AND THIS QUOTE WILL STICK WITH ME FOREVER), WHEN MOM SAID IN THE MESSAGES (AND I AM PARA-PHRASING):

> "JILLIAN MAY GET MAD AT YOU, BUT I AGREE THAT IT IS THE ONLY OPTION THAT YOU HAVE LEFT."

HIS RESPONSE WAS THIS, AND THIS ONE I AM NOT PARAPHRASING:

> "I CAN DEAL WITH THAT. I WOULD RATHER HAVE HER HEALTHY AND BE MAD AT ME."